DAN ANDERSON
A BIOGRAPHY

Dan Anderson in his office, facing the Old Lodge

HAZELDEN'S PIONEERS

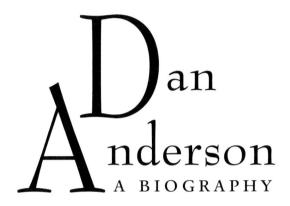

Dan Anderson
A BIOGRAPHY

Damian McElrath, Ph.D.

With a foreword by John Schwarzlose, president and CEO,
Betty Ford Center, Rancho Mirage, California

INFORMATION & EDUCATIONAL SERVICES

Hazelden
Center City, Minnesota 55012-0176
1-800-328-9000
1-651-257-1331 (fax)
www.hazelden.org

© 1999 by Hazelden Foundation
All rights reserved
Printed in the United States of America
No portion of this publication may be reproduced in any manner without the written permission of the publisher.

Library of Congress Cataloging-in-Publication-Data
McElrath, Damian.
    Biography of Dan Anderson / Damian McElrath.
      p. cm. — (Hazelden's Pioneers)
    Includes bibliographical references and index.
    ISBN 1-56838-310-X
      1. Hazelden Foundation—History. 2. Anderson, Dan, 1921 - . 3. Drug abuse counselors—United States—Biography. 4. Alcoholism counselors—United States—Biography. 5. Substance abuse—Treatment—Minnesota—History. I. Title. II Series.
HV5281.H39M38   1998
262.29' 186' 092—dc21   98-35225
[B]   CIP

02 01 00 99 5 4 3 2 1

Cover design by David Spohn
Interior design by Nora Koch, Gravel Pit Publications
Typesetting by Nora Koch, Gravel Pit Publications

Special thanks to editor Gretchen Bratvold

PHOTO CREDITS

p. 2 (Dan Anderson as a toddler and young boy); p. 6 (Dan and Marie Anderson, 1956); p. 10 (Dan Anderson in U.S. Army); p. 34, 35 (photos of the Anderson family); p. 46 (Dan Anderson, Pat Butler, and others at Hazelden groundbreaking ceremony, 1964); p. 80 (Dan Anderson on sailboat); p. 94 (Dan and Marie Anderson)
—*Anderson Family Collection*

Frontispiece (Dan Anderson, facing the Old Lodge); p. x (Damian McElrath, Betty Ford, and Dan Anderson); p. 8 (Dan Anderson speaking at groundbreaking ceremony, expansion of Fellowship Club, 1978); p. 14 (Dan Anderson expressing an idea before two interested onlookers); p. 22 (Nelson Bradley); p. 31 (Pat Butler, Will Foster, and Dan Anderson); p. 49 (Dan Anderson departing for Russia, 1986); p. 58 (photos of Dan Anderson giving speeches); p. 61 (The Old Lodge and Hazelden's modern treatment units); p. 64 (Gordon Grimm. Others pictured are models, not actual patients); p. 69 (Lynn Carroll); p. 72 (Dan Anderson at Hazelden board meeting); p. 108 (Dan Anderson); p. 134 (Dan Anderson)
—*Hazelden Pittman Archives*

CONTENTS

Foreword by John Schwarzlose	ix
Introduction	xvii
1: Youth	1
2: Education and Interest in Psychology	13
3: The Willmar Experience: The Roots of the Minnesota Model	21
4: The Bridge to Hazelden	45
5: Changes at Center City	57
6: Evolution of the Multidisciplinary Team	71
7: Challenges at Hazelden	79
8: Reflections on the Past, Present, and Future	93
Bibliography	103
Appendixes: Dan Anderson's Selected Essays	
Appendix 1: *The Psychopathology of Denial*	107
Appendix 2: From *Behavioral Management of Chronic Illness*	133
About the Author	171

Foreword

by
John Schwarzlose, president and CEO of the
Betty Ford Center, Rancho Mirage, California

(Left to right) Damian McElrath, former First Lady Betty Ford, and Dan Anderson during Mrs. Ford's visit to Hazelden in April 1980

Nearly half a century has passed since Dan Anderson, Nelson Bradley, and their colleagues began work at Minnesota's Willmar State Hospital on a new model for treating alcoholism. Acknowledging that current methods simply weren't working, these pioneers set out to develop a more effective one. Their contributions, which were nothing less than revolutionary, gave birth to what is today known as the Minnesota Model for alcoholism treatment. The result of their work has subsequently made an enormous difference in the lives of millions of people.

Let's fast-forward to 1980. Former First Lady Betty Ford and Leonard Firestone, who were both in recovery, had decided to establish a treatment center in southern California. They chose a special place for it in the desert near the San Jacinto Mountains, a beautiful and peaceful site free of distraction, an ideal place to begin a healing journey. Their goal was to create a treatment program that would be as special and unique as the land on which it was located.

Betty and Leonard began the project by talking with leaders in the addiction treatment field and visiting various treatment centers throughout the country. By 1980, Hazelden was the preeminent leader in addiction treatment, and Dan had been working there for nearly twenty years when he agreed to talk with Betty and Leonard. After visiting Hazelden and talking with Dan and Pat Butler, they returned to California convinced that they ought to try to emulate Hazelden's model: carefully managed, professional treatment carried out in a supportive and nurturing environment. Betty and Leonard had been very impressed that Dan had not put on a full-court sales pitch. Though they didn't yet know it, Dan's style is anything but that. He had helped Betty and Leonard get a feel for Hazelden's magic and heart, and that's what they came away wanting to recreate.

Some in Dan's position would have seen the Betty Ford Center as a potential threat to Hazelden's preeminence. Dan's reaction, however, was not only to graciously agree to help, but to encourage them to improve on what Hazelden had done. When he learned, for example, that Betty and Leonard had been able to convince the California legislature to grant the Betty Ford Center a special license as a chemical dependency recovery hospital, he encouraged them to develop and include a strong medical component in their program. Dan knew that with such a license, they could move beyond what Hazelden was able to do in this area. Dan strove to help Betty and Leonard create the best treatment center possible. That some aspects of their center's program might improve on Hazelden's did not matter to him.

When we opened the Betty Ford Center in 1982, Mrs. Ford and I wanted to maintain our relationship with Dan, so we invited him to spend two to four weeks each winter at the center as a consultant and help us evaluate our program. Not long after that, Dan gave us one of many examples of how valuable his insight is. Sitting down one day with Betty and me, Dan said, "I can already see that you're going to be another Hazelden, another of the stand-out treatment programs people will want to go to. And . . . well . . . so what."

Betty and I looked at each other, both wondering what he was driving at.

Dan paused a few moments longer and then said, "Betty. John. Think of the position you're in. The Betty Ford Center was founded by a woman, a former first lady, a person who had the courage to come out in the open while in the White House and talk about her breast cancer. And then this same woman again shocked our country some years later when she publicly stated that she was going into treatment for alcoholism and medication addiction. The Betty Ford Center can and should be more than just another excellent treatment center. It should become the number one treatment center for women in the United States. You, Betty, are a spokesperson for women in this country; take advantage of this."

Our subsequent success in treating women is due to the efforts of not only Betty, but all of our staff. Both she and I, however, give much credit to Dan Anderson, who was here at the right time to help us see our potential and to give us the push we needed to take advantage of the opportunity we had to help women. In the years that followed, Dan's experience in the field and his astute advice on program and financial matters have helped the Betty Ford Center make some very wise business decisions that have enabled us to maintain a sound economic footing too.

The Betty Ford Center has worked with consultants in many areas, but none compare to Dan Anderson. He is very perceptive, yet very unassuming. To say what he's meant to the Betty Ford Center is very difficult. He is a consultant in the best sense of the word, and a colleague. And he continues to be more than a friend. I have long told people, and proudly, I might add, that Dan Anderson is my mentor. Not so long ago, Betty heard me acknowledge this in a speech. Afterwards, she came to me and said, "John, I want to tell you that in many ways, Dan has been my mentor too."

It's clear that Dan Anderson has always had the best interests of patients at heart in his work. With Dan's help, we have been able to bring the spirit of Hazelden to this center. Certainly there are differences in our organizations, but there are many similarities too. By helping the Betty Ford Center be the best it can be, he has helped ensure that the individuals who come here for treatment will receive the best that we can possibly give them, and this is a tribute to all that Hazelden and Dan have done.

Introduction

The name Dan Anderson will be readily known to those who are familiar with Hazelden and the Minnesota Model of treatment for chemical dependency. For those unacquainted with the development of this model, the subsequent pages will enlighten you. While much of Anderson's reputation derives from his role as one of the founders of the renowned Minnesota Model, his continuing public advocacy of it as a remedy for the illness that afflicts the lives of so many individuals and families must not go unnoticed. He was tireless in his efforts to educate the public about the nature of the illness and was adept at translating the nature and character of the Minnesota Model for the professional—doctors, psychologists, clergy, social workers, educators—as well as for the nonprofessional.

Initially Anderson was both ignorant and suspicious of Alcoholics Anonymous (AA), wrongly identifying it with the religious character of the Salvation Army. It did not take long, however, before he was convinced of the value of the AA program and principles as well as the enviable power it possessed in keeping people sober. He helped

Introduction

thousands of others to understand the importance of the movement. His commitment was unwavering, and those who had him in the classroom at the Rutgers Summer School of Alcohol Studies or in training at Hazelden or anywhere else came away respecting and understanding the nature of the illness of chemical dependency and the effectiveness of treatment according to the Minnesota Model.

Besides being an educator and translator, Anderson was also a visionary. People were mesmerized by the breadth and depth of his ideas. All who encountered him at Hazelden came away amazed at how generous he was with his time and thoughts for the present and future of the field. Perhaps inevitably, some colleagues on the home front grumbled that he was giving away the store, for those outside Hazelden who listened to him went away and implemented what he was teaching them.

Anderson loved to experiment, to cultivate and hatch new ideas, and Hazelden was the laboratory for his concepts. He was primarily responsible for the growth of the continuum of care that extended beyond primary treatment. Evaluation was crucial to his way of thinking, for it told him what to discard and what to cherish. He was a zealous advocate of prevention, of health promotion, and of treating other chronic illnesses beyond chemical dependency. Anderson believed that Hazelden's future goal was to help improve the lifestyle of anyone who came in contact with Hazelden—not only to prevent chronic diseases in young people, but also to teach people of all ages to change their lives in positive ways. Most important, Anderson was not afraid of change. When he retired from the presidency of Hazelden in 1986, he left the treatment center with an outstanding legacy. Many of his ideas, too novel for his colleagues and contemporaries, are now being implemented.

The following biographical sketch highlights the confluence of factors that led to Anderson's involvement with alcoholics and the care and compassion that he demonstrated for them. Anderson's parents, his early travels, his education and inclination toward psychology, his wife, friends, and colleagues all influenced the path he chose in life and especially the installation and growth of the Minnesota Model at Hazelden.

DAN ANDERSON
A BIOGRAPHY

1
Youth

Dan Anderson as a toddler (above) and young boy (right). His streak of rebelliousness against the conventional way of doing things can be traced back as far as his birth in 1921.

One of Dan Anderson's finest traits was his willingness to test the waters, to go beyond the accepted, to try the new and the challenging, and in the process breathe confidence into the timid, energize the reluctant, inspire the doubter, and carry along in his wake those who shared his enthusiasm and excitement for exploring new horizons. Accompanying that trait was a streak of rebelliousness against the conventional way of doing things that could be traced as far back as his birth, which occurred on March 30, 1921, in northeast Minneapolis. In fact, Anderson's unconventional birth was the cause of great concern during his mother's extremely difficult three-day labor, an event that was noted in the local Minneapolis paper. During the prolonged delivery, the doctor, suffering from worry and fatigue, had asked Dan's father whom he should save in the worst possible scenario that only one would survive. Dan's father replied, "My wife—we can always have another child." Despite this initial rejection, Dan and his father became extremely close during the relatively short time they would have together.

Dan's father, Arvid John Anderson, and his mother,

Evelyn de Pugh, were married in 1919 in a civil ceremony, followed a year later by a formal religious ceremony in a Catholic church, the religion of his mother. Arvid was of Swedish origin, had a younger sister named Florence, belonged to a Masonic order, and worked for Northwestern Bell Telephone Company. Evelyn was one of three daughters from a poor family of Irish descent and a strict and devout Catholic. Dan's father converted to Catholicism when Dan was about ten years old. Dan perceived his father to be a "reasonable" Catholic, in contrast to his mother's intense piety and a propensity toward the rigidity that many Irish Americans manifested in the first half of the twentieth century. As with most Irish families, especially with the women, the expectation in Dan's family was that the firstborn son would become a priest. His mother required that he memorize the Baltimore catechism, say his rosary and prayers at her knees, and attend Mass without fail. She was also good at laying the formidable Celtic-Catholic guilt trip on young Dan, stressing that unless he were good, God might punish the family by taking his father at an early age. Dan's father was more realistic about it. Having suffered lung and heart damage as a result of the inhalation of mustard gas in World War I, Arvid wanted his son to grow up as quickly as possible so that when he died, Dan would be ready to care for his mother and two sisters, Colleen and

Dawn, who were born in 1924 and 1934, respectively.

Both parents influenced their son profoundly but in different ways. From his mother, Dan inherited a deep and abiding faith, love, and respect for the mysteries of Catholicism, especially the sacraments and the Mass. From his father, Dan gained a singular humanitarianism that manifested itself in an innate kindness toward the poor and the underprivileged. Often Dan watched his father splicing telephone cables in a poor neighborhood, giving the little children odd jobs such as putting sleeves over the wires to seal them together. Not only did the children feel useful by helping Arvid, but also they were overjoyed when he would reward them with a penny. This regard for the poor and the underprivileged served as a model for Dan, as he later became more and more interested in the world of deviancy—the world of the alcoholic.

Dan often relates with tongue in cheek that his proclivity toward deviation and pathology accompanied by his sensitivity to the addict and the afflicted might be attributed to the fact that he was born with a wry neck, which caused him to see others and the world from an angled position. He was five years old when he had corrective surgery, and he remembers the subsequent therapy to correct the condition—being "hung" by his neck at the Shriner's Hospital in St. Paul.

After a year at a public school, Dan transferred to

One of Dan Anderson's finest traits was to test the waters, and here he is doing just that with wife, Marie, 1956.

Ascension Catholic in north Minneapolis. While he was still in the eighth grade at Ascension, Dan's mother died unexpectedly due to complications from childbirth, soon after giving birth to his second sister, Dawn, in 1934. Shortly thereafter, Dan's father, forty at the time and worried about the children, married his wife's sister's daughter, Evelyn Crevier, who was only nineteen years old. Dan's father died a year and a half later, in 1936, while Dan was in his first year of high school at St. Thomas Military Academy.

It was understandable that the young stepmother found the task of caring for three children, one of whom was just a baby, beyond her strength. Dan and his sister Connie (Colleen) were sent to relatives in the small town of Williams, one of Minnesota's most remote outposts, while Evelyn kept Dawn with her. It was a remarkable contrast to the Twin Cities, and Dan had to adapt to a rural culture. He donned their clothes and learned how to roll his own cigarettes. Since it was the decade of the Great Depression, money was scarce and Dan had very little. At the age of sixteen, he took a job tending bar at the Idle Hours Cafe, where he earned the nickname "Hard Cash" because his employer never saw him spend any money. While pouring drinks and shaking California dice, Dan listened to the stories of idle patrons. Williams, Minnesota, was peppered with old men living on their claims who came to the Idle

Dan in 1978, speaking at the groundbreaking ceremony for the expansion of Fellowship Club. He spent much of his youth learning at "the college of human experience"—riding with truckers, mingling with men from all walks of life, including drunkards—which proved invaluable for the avocation he eventually chose.

Hours Cafe to share their wisdom with the young bartender. When Dan asked one of them what advice he could give, his laconic response was, "Very few people get out of this world alive." Dan wondered to himself, "My God, is this all [the wisdom] there is?"

Catholic Mass in the small town was every other Sunday. In the winter on the nights before Mass, Dan would walk a mile to the church in the biting cold after work to start and tend the fire during the early morning hours until it was time for the priest to begin Mass. Throughout his life, Dan never missed Sunday Mass if he could help it.

After a couple of years, his stepmother wanted the two children back, and Dan and Colleen went to live with her in a small cottage off Lake Minnetonka. Dan finished high school second lowest in the class. He had actually wagered that he would come in last. It was common knowledge that he did not like school, but he loved to read and would spend hours in the library reading books and perusing the periodicals. Favorites on his reading list were *The New Yorker* and *National Geographic*. He was attracted to girls too much to fulfill his mother's wishes that he become a priest. He wasn't into competitive athletics, but he liked to sail Lake Minnetonka, savoring the solitude it afforded him. In his high school yearbook he was given the nickname "Sleepy" for his reputation of sleeping with his head on his desk when he had stayed out late the night before.

Dan Anderson, U.S. Army during World War II

Shortly after completing high school in 1939, Anderson went "on the bum," riding freight trains to Chicago, where he visited the World's Fair, and then to Seattle. From others he quickly learned the important lesson of lying down on top of the freight car when the lace hit. These telltale chains suspended over the tracks before a tunnel warned railroad bums of dire consequences if they did not lie flat.

In Seattle, hungry, unwashed, and broke, he managed to gain entrance into a home for Jewish emigrants. Despite his best efforts to conceal his background, it was not long before it was discovered that he was not Jewish, but Scandinavian and Irish. Having been gently eased out of the shelter, he walked the Seattle docks and sought unsuccessfully to enlist on the *Takoma*, a Hamburg-American lines' tender that supplied the famous World War II battleship the *Graf Spee*. He then hitchhiked to California, where he picked fruit and hops, at times being cheated of his full wages, living in jungle camps, riding with truckers, and mingling with men from all walks of life, including drunkards. This was the college of human experience, which would prove invaluable to the young Anderson for the avocation that he eventually chose.

Anderson returned to the Twin Cities in December 1939 and lived with his grandmother in northeast Minneapolis. War had broken out in Europe after Hitler's *Wehrmacht* invaded Poland. The young Anderson wanted to enlist in the Royal Canadian Air Force, which had already joined the war effort, but he was rejected because of poor eyesight. After Pearl Harbor, Anderson was drafted into the U.S. Army in June 1942 and was taught how to operate fire-control radar for antiaircraft guns. The division to which he was assigned had the task of protecting Allied airfields throughout the Southwest Pacific, and his outfit set up the protective umbrella for the U.S. Air Force after the capture of the Solomon Islands. In October 1945, at the termination of the war, Anderson was given an honorable discharge, having attained the rank of staff sergeant.

The war, another in a long series of demonstrations in world history of man's inhumanity to man, only increased Anderson's cynicism about his fellow human beings who composed the conventional world—a world that, despite the popularized postwar view, rang pretty hollow for many of the returning veterans. Anderson resented that his discharge papers described him as a common laborer. Indeed, this became one of the compelling factors in his decision to go to college.

2
Education and Interest in Psychology

Dan Anderson (center) expressing an idea before two interested Hazelden board members. Many have noted that people were mesmerized by the breadth and depth of Anderson's ideas.

While he did not consider himself a ditchdigger, Anderson had difficulty determining what he wanted to be. When asked, he would sardonically reply, "I would like to be an interesting conversationalist at afternoon cocktail parties." Availing himself of the GI Bill of Rights to subsidize his education, Anderson selected the College of St. Thomas in St. Paul and managed to convince the admissions personnel that he was an acceptable candidate even though his high school grades had been low and he lacked certain credits.

To earn some extra pocket money, Anderson worked the soda fountain at the Walgreen's in downtown Minneapolis for $32 a week. One of his co-workers was a pretty teenager, ten years younger than he. Her name was Marie Wedekind, a sophomore at North High School. The oldest of five children, Marie was born on November 27, 1931, nine miles from Hackensack, Minnesota, located along Big Deep Lake. She was twelve years old when her family moved to north Minneapolis. She was attracted to Dan because of his great sense of humor and his deep compassion for the poor and deprived. One incident indelibly imprinted in her memory was the time that Dan gave a person in need at the drugstore $20 for food and lodging, more than half his weekly salary. But at the same time she also recognized his cynicism, sarcasm, and rebelliousness.

Marie was surprised but delighted when Dan asked her out. She never thought that he would be interested in her because he was so much older than she and because he and another collegian teased her, a few times so unmercifully, in fact, that she broke into tears publicly. At the sight of Marie crying, Dan became embarrassed and apologetic. After work they would walk around downtown Minneapolis, then Dan would escort her home and walk the four miles back to his own room.

In 1947, a class field trip to Hastings State Hospital turned Anderson's attention toward psychology, the field in which he would receive his bachelor of arts degree. While the experience of being in a hospital with nine hundred mentally ill patients at first frightened Dan, it also left him deeply impressed with the suffering he witnessed. While still young and cynical, he occasionally observed aloud in front of others that there was more truth in a nuthouse than in the world outside.

When Anderson discovered that he could work at Hastings for double the wages he received at Walgreen's and receive room and board as well, he decided to change jobs. In September 1948 he moved to Hastings and made the third floor of one of the patient cottages his new home. When not attending classes at St. Thomas, Anderson performed the general duties of a psychiatric aide in various patient cottages as well as in the hospital and the surgery wards. A major drawback was that he now lived farther away from Marie. She made the round-trip to Hastings by bus so that they could spend about four hours together on a Saturday or Sunday.

The residency at Hastings was a marvelous experience for Anderson. He was introduced to the world of mental illness, schizophrenia, electric shock, and prefrontal lobotomies. It was the world of the snake pit. In spite of the conditions, Anderson spent a great deal of time with the patients. He gradually found it easy to talk to them, and he soon discovered that he liked them. He had inherited his father's compassion for the deprived and the neglected, the societal misfits. This was the beginning of his attraction to the world of behavior pathology, in particular his fascination with the world of schizophrenics. At this time, he knew nothing about alcoholics, although he suspected some of the staff at Hastings were borderline cases.

With his interest in psychology firmly in place, Anderson graduated cum laude from the College of St. Thomas in 1950, quite a transformation and achievement for the student who graduated from high school next to the bottom of the class. He was offered a job as secretary to the state commissioner of mental health, but someone else had already entered his life who, second only to Marie, was to have a profound influence on him and his future.

In 1947 a young physician named Nelson Bradley had been driving from Saskatchewan, Canada, to a hospital in Michigan for a surgical residency. His car broke down in the Twin Cities. During the following week, Bradley spent some time on the campus of the University of Minnesota, where by chance he met Dr. Ralph Rossen, the superintendent at Hastings State Hospital. Rossen talked Bradley into changing his plans and coming to work as a physician at Hastings, where he met Dan Anderson. The two became the closest of friends. In Bradley, Anderson found a kindred spirit, skeptical of the institutional manner in which patients were treated. Both were influenced by the progressive ideas of Rossen. Rossen was guided by a simple theme, namely, to focus on each single day in the life of a patient, always trying to improve the quality of that patient's life. This was the inspiration and model that Bradley and Anderson would follow as they sought to humanize demeaning systems of treatment, respecting the dignity of each patient and helping patients in nonconventional ways.

In 1950, the year Anderson graduated from St. Thomas, Bradley was appointed superintendent of Willmar State

Hospital, and Rossen was promoted to serve as the state commissioner of mental health and was transferred to St. Paul. Rossen offered Anderson a job as his secretary in the St. Paul office, but Anderson did not relish the idea of pushing a pen and being confined to an office. He liked working directly with patients, and, besides, he couldn't type. While Anderson was contemplating Rossen's offer, Bradley persuaded Anderson to move to Willmar with him and take a position as recreation worker at $200 a month—"the low man on the totem pole," as Anderson later described it. Although Anderson was uncertain about the nature of his new position, he looked forward to continuing his professional relationship with Bradley. Life with Bradley promised to be much more exciting than sitting in an office all day. One drawback, however, was that Willmar was even farther away from Marie. In the following months, either Marie would travel there by train or Dan would drive down and back in his dilapidated secondhand car, uncertain whether it would expire at any moment in the journey.

Bradley told Anderson that Willmar had 1,800 beds, "Still a snake pit, but I think we can fix it up. They also have thirty to forty 'inebs' [inebriates] there." He then asked Anderson if he knew anything about inebs. Anderson said no, but, typical of a recent college graduate, he added, "We'll look it up though and see what it is."

Nonetheless, Anderson realized that in order to help Bradley and be accepted by the staff he would have to further his education. He was accepted at Loyola University in Chicago for the fall semester in 1950 as a clinical psychology major. He had to borrow most of his tuition, because only a little remained of his GI bill. During his two semesters at Loyola he took the bread-and-butter psychology courses in testing and report writing. He liked applied psychology but disliked Chicago. He was lonely, he missed Marie, and he was poor. To help cut expenses, he shared an apartment with two other students and did the grocery shopping and cooking to make certain that they remained within the meager resources the three of them had pooled.

Marie typed his master's thesis, which was the beginning of her doing all of Dan's typing; after completing his course work for his master's degree, Anderson returned to Willmar in the summer of 1951. Because he had not completed his dissertation, Anderson was employed as an intern psychologist at $160 a month—less than he had earned as a recreation worker. His supervisor, Roy Miller, told him that he was going to work with the inebriates and that after six months he would graduate and work with the "real" patients. He began to search out and read literature on the treatment of alcoholics, but there wasn't much available. He and Bradley were the only ones who really liked working with them.

3

The Willmar Experience: The Roots of the Minnesota Model

Nelson Bradley at Willmar State Hospital. Bradley and Anderson were true pioneers in their efforts to humanize systems of treatment—respecting the dignity of each patient and helping patients in nonconventional ways, which became the basis for the Hazelden treatment model.

After Anderson returned to Willmar, he and Marie finally ended their long-distance courtship and married on June 13, 1953. After honeymooning in Grand Lake, Colorado, they settled in Willmar in an apartment over the admissions office at the hospital. At Willmar, Marie and Dan Anderson became lifelong friends with Jan and Nelson Bradley, and the two couples spent a great deal of time together, particularly at the Bradley home, where Dan and Nelson would brainstorm until all hours of the night and sometimes into the morning. They were particularly adept at stimulating one another's creativity.

During the next decade, with Willmar as their experimental laboratory, the two men, Bradley the psychiatrist and Anderson the psychologist, formed definite and progressive, even revolutionary, ideas about the treatment of alcoholism. In his position as hospital superintendent, Bradley was able to implement a treatment program that, while simple enough in its content, was radically divergent from the psychiatric methodology and understanding of alcoholism. From the very outset, both Bradley and Anderson felt that the answer to the problem of alcoholism was not to be found in the psychoanalytical theories championed by most psychiatrists at that time. Eventually they decided to abandon both the psychoanalytic approach and the desocialized atmosphere of an institution altogether. But it took some time to put all the revamped pieces in place.

Shortly after his arrival at Willmar, Bradley initiated a series of changes directed toward better care of the alcoholic patients, who were angry about being locked up in the same ward as the mental patients. Bradley instituted an open door policy for them and separated them from the other patients. He intuitively recognized the need to dissociate the alcoholic from the stigma of mental illness, with its corollary of locked wards. He developed a lecture schedule to educate the patients on the symptoms of the various stages of alcoholism. As the lecture series evolved over the years under the direction of Anderson, topics were added on the illness and its multifaceted nature.

E. M. Jellinek and the Center of Alcohol Studies

Anderson based the information in his lecture series at Willmar on the Jellinek Chart, named after Dr. Elvin Morton Jellinek, a scientist who had pioneered research on alcoholism at the Center of Alcohol Studies at Yale University in the late thirties and the forties. From a questionnaire study of members of AA, Jellinek formulated his concept of phases in the drinking history of alcoholics. Later, he administered a more detailed questionnaire to about two thousand alcoholics and presented his analysis of this data and his concept of the phases of alcohol addiction in lectures at the Yale Summer School of Alcohol Studies in July 1951 and 1952, as well as at the European Seminar on Alcoholism in Copenhagen in October 1951. A leader in the movement to recognize alcoholism as a major public health problem, the Center of Alcohol Studies also helped push the American Medical Association (AMA) to accept alcoholism as a treatable illness, a policy the AMA formally adopted in the fifties.

In 1962 the Center of Alcohol Studies moved to Rutgers University, where the Summer School of Alcohol Studies continues to convene annually. The first interdisciplinary research center devoted to alcohol use and its related problems and treatment, the Center of Alcohol Studies has over the years provided consultants and experts for many important organizations and meetings. Today, the Center of Alcohol Studies is known nationally and internationally as a leader in alcohol research, education, and training.

Bradley and Anderson began to bump into a movement called AA. They had little knowledge of it except what they had learned from their brief conversations with Fred Eiden, a recovering alcoholic who worked at Hastings.

But at Hastings alcoholism was not the primary focus. It was not until Bradley and Anderson went to Willmar that the alcoholic population became the object of their immediate attention. Although the two men did not understand AA very well—neither its philosophy nor its comic relief that spiced AA conversations and talks—they intuitively recognized that AA's sense of humor was interwoven with deep spiritual insights. Gradually Bradley and Anderson came to see that AA could sober up alcoholics and sustain them in their recovery. It was also apparent that recovering alcoholics had phenomenal insights into the thinking and personalities of alcoholics. Although the inner workings of AA in those early days at Willmar might have been a mystery to Bradley and Anderson, it was evident that this self-help group worked.

The Rise of AA

AA founders Bill W., a New York stockbroker, and Dr. Bob, a physician from Akron, Ohio, began meeting in May 1935 to help each other overcome their drinking problems. Bill W. had stopped drinking several months previous, and Dr. Bob took his last drink on June 10, 1935. His dry date marks the beginning of AA, though at the time the group had no conscious identity. The impact these two men had on each other made them feel an urgency to help other alcoholics by sharing their own experiences.

At first the growth of the group was slow, with only about a hundred members in the first four years, referred to as the flying-blind period because everything was done on a day-to-day basis, with no Twelve Steps and no Big Book. After the publication of *Alcoholics Anonymous* (the Big Book) in the spring of 1939, members began to adopt the book's name for their group, as well. Orders for the book poured in, and by the end of the year an estimated eight hundred alcoholics were on their way to recovery. Within two more years, at the end of 1941, membership had soared to eight thousand and AA was a national organization. By the nineties, AA had two million members from 114 countries. Most professionals in the field of alcohol and drug treatment now believe that any form of treatment has a higher success rate when the patient simultaneously joins AA. M. Scott Peck (the psychologist, spiritual writer, and author of *The Road Less Traveled*) has identified AA as one of the three most significant spiritual turning points of the twentieth century (the other two being the Holocaust and the Second Vatican Council). Peck noted the power of AA as a model of community that could serve not only individual nations but also the entire global community.

Prior to 1950, professionals had little or no success in dealing with inebriates. They simply did not know what to do with them. Bradley was open to anything that might help. Consequently, he started a tradition of inviting and welcoming speakers from AA groups throughout the state to speak at Willmar. Both the patients and staff attended these talks. Because he was convinced that recovering alcoholics had a special way with "drunks," Bradley hired Mel Brandes, a recovering alcoholic, in 1951. Brandes served as patient placement coordinator, a guise that allowed him to work one-on-one with the alcoholic patients. Other professionals on staff at Willmar would not have approved of Brandes's appointment if they had understood that he would be working directly with patients although he had no professional background.

Bradley and Anderson planted the seeds of the multidisciplinary approach to the treatment of alcoholics in the early fifties. The professionals were rotated in the lecture cycle. The physicians performed the physicals with brief medical and mental histories. And the psychologists occasionally spoke with the patients on an individual basis. Bradley created a very relaxed atmosphere, which helped foster good staff morale as well as a spontaneity that allowed for the staff's willingness and desire to develop new approaches to treatment.

But one important player was missing from the multidisciplinary team, and that was a counselor who knew what alcoholism was all about and who, unlike the undercover role played by Brandes, would be a legitimate and accepted player on the treatment team. Bradley, supported by Anderson, knew that he would have to buck tradition by hiring recovering alcoholics to assist with treatment. In 1953 they approached the Minnesota Civil Service Commission with the request to hire these people as treatment counselors. They were met with scorn and skepticism. But they persisted, and in 1954 John Jackson, the head of the commission, created the position of counselor on alcoholism, thanks to the goodwill of Governor Elmer Anderson. It was a singular moment in the development of the Minnesota Model as well as in the treatment of alcoholism throughout the United States. Minnesota was the first state to create these civil service positions to be part of a professional team.

Since Willmar was the only state hospital in Minnesota to treat alcoholics, the four positions budgeted by the state were allotted to Willmar. Mel Brandes and Lowell Maxwell were hired immediately, followed shortly thereafter by Fred Eiden, Bradley's friend and former co-worker at Hastings. Eiden would become the tutor and mentor of the Willmar staff on the illness of alcoholism and the treatment of alcoholics. Willmar already had in place its physicians, nurses, psychiatrists, psychologists, chaplains, social workers, and recreation directors. Now it also had nondegreed counselors on alcoholism, laypeople expected to share responsibility with the professionals for the treatment program. It is difficult today to imagine how radical a change this was—to go from a physician-oriented, psychoanalytic methodology to a treatment program conducted by "drunks." Of course, it did not happen all at once. The concept was revolutionary, and the process toward a multidisciplinary team was gradual and not without obstacles and resistance.

What the newly hired counselors on alcoholism inherited as a program for the inebriates was about thirty lectures that the professional staff had been delivering on a variety of subjects as well as one-on-one sessions conducted by Mel Brandes with the patients who needed the most help. When Bradley moved the afternoon lectures to the morning, it was a clear signal that structured treatment was more important than work assignments, even though the latter consumed six to eight hours of the patients' day. They would perform tasks in the kitchen, the dining hall, the power house, the office, or outside cleaning up the grounds or working on the farm. The idea was that it was important to keep the alcoholics working, even though they were not paid. But lectures and group now became the heart and soul of the program, with one-on-ones assigned as the patient requested or as the counselor deemed necessary. Each of the counselors had about thirty patients. Their style was caring and nonconfrontational, and the content simple and uncomplicated. The group talked about the Twelve Steps, particularly the substance

Dan (at right) with Pat Butler (left) and Will Foster, director of the National Institute on Alcohol Abuse and Alcoholism, during Foster's visit to Hazelden in 1980

of the First Step, powerlessness and unmanageability, addressed specifically to those members who were finding it difficult or impossible to accept their personal loss of control and recognize the harmful consequences that resulted from their drinking.

Over the course of the subsequent years, Eiden emerged as the acknowledged master, mentor, and model for Willmar's rehabilitation program for the alcoholic. There was no logic or strategic plan for the development of the multidisciplinary team. Initially, there were no formal staff teams for individual patients and very little planned collaboration. There was a great deal of informal conversation, first among the professionals themselves, and second, between them and Eiden in the coffee shop or in their offices. Eiden was at his best in this informal educative process. When not modeling for the professionals by working his own AA program, informally he was explaining, exhorting, cajoling, and patiently bringing along his wondering colleagues to examine, understand, and accept alcoholism as a primary illness. Gradually the mystery of the addictive need finally got through to the professionals. Some began to understand the mystery, others did not, but all commenced to recognize its presence.

Anderson confronted the mystery early on, before he went to Ottowa to continue his studies. He recalled:

I can remember the first year of Fred's arrival. While working with alcoholics who had terrible psychological problems, after shrinking their heads, I watched them get well right in front of me. They would thank me, shake my hand, and say that they were going home—only to wind up back at Willmar again. This same patient would apologize to me saying that I had really helped him so much the last time. He really appreciated that and did feel better, but nonetheless he was still drinking. He would then add, "This time I think I'd better see what is going on in the AA program."

Another person who was to have a great influence on Dan Anderson was Patrick Butler, one of the Saturday night speakers at Willmar. In 1951 the Butler family decided to provide the financial backing for the floundering Hazelden enterprise, which had opened its doors in Center City in 1949 as a residential facility for treating alcoholics in a serene and caring environment. Pat Butler invited Anderson and Bradley to his home on Summit Avenue in St. Paul, where they became frequent visitors. The three of them would spend hours talking about AA and alcoholism. Butler intuited that at Willmar they were up to something that made eminent sense in the treatment of alcoholics. They, for their part, took advantage of Butler's offer to borrow from his library any of the many books that he had on the subject of alcoholism. Anderson recalls

The early days of the Anderson family . . .

Dan and Marie with children

Marie, holding baby Doug, and children

Dan and children sitting at the doorstep to their apartment in Ottawa during the time when Dan was studying for his Ph.D.

Dan and his children swimming at Sibley Park near New London, Minnesota

Anderson family photo, 1992. Back row (left to right): Monica, Colleen, Cheryl, Dennis, David, Dean, Patti. Front (left to right): Doug, Marie, Dan, Corinne, Cindi.

that at that time Butler was one of the few people in the country who viewed the problem of alcoholism as a general public health concern. In this sense Butler was a visionary, one who could transfer the problem from a very personal one to a societywide, public-policy level.

Turning Pessimism into Opportunity:
Social Climate of the Fifties

The events at Willmar occurred at a time when there was great pessimism and even despair about the possibility of recovery for alcoholics. Their high death rate precluded optimism. The social stigma surrounding alcoholics also enveloped the people associated with them or seeking to help them. Even the mental patients looked down upon the inebs similar to the way that alcoholics would later look down upon those who ingested pills. Trying to change attitudes about alcoholism was time-consuming and taxing. Marie Anderson remembers how in the early days Dan would come home frustrated after having given a lecture to a community group on the concept of alcoholism as an illness. Many people, in particular religious temperance groups, were not ready for it.

It is in this social context and because of it that the Willmar experience became such a rich and rewarding phenomenon. First Willmar, under Bradley's leadership, and then Hazelden, under

Anderson's and Butler's leadership, began and continued the process of raising the nation's consciousness about the rehabilitation of alcoholics; namely, that they should not be stigmatized or looked down upon because of their illness. Humane treatment was possible when facilitated by a multidisciplinary team in an intensive treatment setting and with a caring community of fellow sufferers. Bradley, Anderson, and Butler were determined to help alcoholics as long as science had not found a solution. The caring community concept evolved from their own compassion for the poor and the abandoned.

Having gone to the Yale Summer School of Alcohol Studies himself for the past several years, Butler paid Anderson's way in 1954. The summer school had a lasting influence on Anderson. He initiated the course on alcohol rehabilitation at Yale in 1959 and lectured that year and the following. After the alcohol program was transferred to Rutgers in 1962, Anderson continued to lecture there for the next three decades. Selden Bacon and his colleagues at the summer school were furthering the understanding of alcoholism through research and scientific papers. After his first experience at Yale, Anderson felt the need to continue his education. Butler generously offered to pay for Anderson's doctoral studies.

In 1955 Anderson, influenced by Jean Rossi, one of the psychologists at Willmar, chose the University of Ottowa in Canada because of its emphasis on clinical psychology. What further attracted Anderson was the specialty in Thomism, the medieval philosophy of St. Thomas Aquinas, who sought to synthesize the powers of reason and philosophical thinking with those of revelation and Christian faith. Anderson had returned from World War II with a cynical attitude toward life. He was skeptical about the possibility of ever arriving at the truth. Aristotle's metaphysics and Aquinas's rational demonstration of the existence of God cast the seeds of doubt about Anderson's premise that, if the truth be told, there can be no truth.

As he moved toward an advanced degree in psychology, Anderson was concerned that at a secular university the orientation to behavioral pathology would be heavily Freudian. He wanted to study clinical psychology within a Christian tradition. In the case of Ottowa this meant within a Thomistic framework. Anderson's curiosity about Aquinas, which had begun with courses as an undergraduate at St. Thomas, continued throughout his life. In the beginning of his *The Joys and Sorrows of Sobriety*, Anderson wrote:

In a memorable passage from the preface to the Summa Theologica, *Thomas Aquinas reflects that "the road that stretches before the feet of a man is a challenge to his heart long before it tests the strength of his legs. Our destiny is to run to the edge of the world and beyond, off into the darkness: sure for all our blindness, secure for all our helplessness, strong for all our weakness, gaily in love for all the pressure on our hearts."*

In addition to a curriculum that Anderson found attractive, another benefit at Ottowa was that tuition was not expensive. Dan, Marie, and their two young children, Dennis and Patricia, moved to Ottowa, where they managed to live very simply and frugally on $350 a month. Despite living on a shoestring these were happy years. The Andersons did have an old car, but they could not afford a TV. When Anderson wasn't tied up with schoolwork, he enjoyed picnics with his family in the mountains or by the rivers, as well as the social gatherings organized by the dean of the psychology department, Father Ray Shevenell, who became a lifelong friend. Dan and Marie arrived with two children and two years later left with two more, Colleen and David, which further constrained their finances. Unlike Chicago, however, Ottowa made Anderson content and gave him the opportunity to work with real patients—embassy staff or students from other countries who needed psychological counseling.

During Anderson's absence from Willmar, Bradley became more and more concerned about the recovering alcoholics who left the structured setting and support of

Willmar. The good prospects and hopes for a continuing recovery needed another component, namely a solid aftercare (now called continuing care). Recovery really took place upon discharge from the treatment program. (Pat Butler had already begun such a program in 1953, when he started Fellowship Club.)

Anderson and his wife returned to Willmar in 1957 and rented an apartment in New London, about twelve miles from the hospital. Two years later they decided that they needed their own home, closer to the hospital, for themselves and their growing family. Upon Anderson's return to Willmar, Bradley appointed him director of the Willmar Alcoholic Follow-Up Clinic at the hospital. So many Willmar graduates came back that Anderson could hardly keep up with the work. He trained two social workers to serve as aftercare counselors in the Twin Cities. He was very careful to select people who understood the nature of the illness and with whom the recovering people could feel comfortable.

The year Anderson returned to Willmar, Bradley decided to take a sabbatical to finish his work for his psychiatric license. He was replaced by another psychiatrist from the Menninger Institute in Kansas who approached the treatment of alcoholism from a psychoanalytic viewpoint. But fortunately, and to the great relief of the staff, he did not interfere with the integration process that was evolving.

Anderson, to whom Bradley had entrusted the lecture series, was allowed to continue the development of the series, which he later installed at Hazelden and which became the principal educational tool for the patients.

Exciting things were taking place in 1957. In addition to the aftercare program, the multidisciplinary concept was beginning to take shape. By the time Anderson returned to Willmar, the staff was really beginning to pull together. The team found itself sharing patients. The jealousy and turf associated with "my patient" were abandoned in the common dispensation of care. The superfluous perquisites of professionalism were dropped almost naturally. This was a first and a remarkable revolution in the history of the human services delivery system.

Anderson aptly illustrated the uniqueness of what was happening. When he returned from Ottowa, he began evaluating selected patients with a battery of tests, including the Minnesota Multiphasic Personality Inventory (MMPI), the results of which he would share with Eiden. The conversations between the two were diagnostic classics. Anderson recalled that he would read the "tea leaves" (the MMPI results) of a patient and would see schizophrenia or an assortment of other disorders. He would then comment to Eiden, "Fred, this one's a real sick one."

Eiden would say something like, "I don't know, Dan, he seems to be getting the program."

In the beginning that did not mean a thing to Anderson. He remembered thinking, "When one is that disturbed, what did it mean 'to get the program'?" And who would win out? Fred would win if this crazy guy remained sober.

On another occasion Anderson recalled, "I would see a guy who was well. I tested him and said to Fred, 'Fred, he's in good shape—not crazy—intelligent and should be a great surgeon someday' (or something to that effect). Fred would say, 'He doesn't have the program though, Dan.'"

This story aptly illustrates the relationship between the recovering counselor and the psychologist, one of the most important members of the multidisciplinary team. Over the years the relationship between the professionals and the recovering counselors would run the gamut from friendly dialogue about the patient's needs, to low-level tension between the two, to an all-out power struggle for the control of the patient's treatment plan and process. History paints many nuances. In a sense the tension between the two revolved around the nature of the craziness that the patient exhibited. Many times the crazy behavior evaporated as the recovery process took hold. In some instances it did not. Over the course of many years, the recovering counselors gradually began to accept the possibility and implications of a dual diagnosis, in which some patients had a mental illness in addition to alcoholism. Told with a sense of humility and humor, Anderson's anecdote, when scrutinized closely, reveals the heart of the matter. The developing Minnesota Model needed to maintain the focus on alcoholism as a complex multiphasic illness that required a multidisciplinary treatment staff, whose primary purpose had to be on arresting the addiction.

With the return of Bradley in 1958 the creative energy was ignited once again. By 1959 Willmar had installed a formal counselor training program supervised by Anderson, a formal pastoral training program supervised by John Keller, and a modest research department in which Anderson played an important role. The decade of the fifties at Willmar State Hospital saw the beginning of the alcoholism treatment revolution. The energy level at the hospital was extremely high. Enthusiasm abounded, and the people involved were caring, innovative, open, bright, and in many ways prophetic. Unlike the staff at Yale, those at Willmar did not resemble a scientific group of researchers but rather a deeply knit community, bound together by care and compassion for a population traditionally treated as parasites or pariahs.

From the time that Anderson returned to Willmar in 1957 until he left in 1961, the hospital experienced an exciting period full of exhilarating events, creative ideas, and wonderful relationships. The staff was in a crisis a great deal of the time, and they led a scrambling sort of existence. The people involved were never quite sure of what they were doing or where they were going with their program. Many of the essential parts of the Minnesota Model developed quite by accident. The planning strategy was situational, scurrying from one task or meeting to the next. But marvelous things were accomplished, and in the minds of those who were a part of them, those days sadly will never return.

Recollecting the events of that period, Bradley summed them up in 1974: "The enthusiasm we had was really something—besides the energy. Everyone was caught up in this. We ate and slept it. We talked about it in the coffee shop—we never let go of it. Now it's like another field. People come into it, and of course they are interested. But, as you say, they learn about it four times more slowly."

4
The Bridge to Hazelden

Dan Anderson (with shovel) and Pat Butler (holding umbrella) during Hazelden's 1964 groundbreaking ceremony for building expansion

During the mid-fifties Pat Butler at Hazelden had been observing the developments at Willmar with growing interest. In 1957 he invited Anderson to spend some time at Hazelden with the patients. Anderson agreed to devote every other Saturday to Hazelden in Center City, giving two lectures and interpreting the psychological testing for the patients. Dia Linn, Hazelden's treatment center for women, had opened in 1956, and these patients were bused to Center City when Anderson visited. The patients enjoyed Anderson's lectures and liked the MMPI interviews, especially when they discovered that they were not mentally ill.

Lynn Carroll was the director of treatment at Center City, a position he had held since Hazelden's inception in 1949. Endowed with great oratorical skills and style and renowned for his practice of the principles and program of AA, Carroll was the principal lecturer and would hold forth from his famous chair in the library for anywhere from half an hour to three hours on the Steps of AA. Pat Butler had only limited success when he repeatedly asked Carroll to stand when he lectured and to limit his talks to half an hour. In the beginning Carroll was pleasant enough to Anderson, but for the most part Carroll ignored Anderson or was absent on the Saturdays when Anderson was there.

Pat Butler's Influence

Pat Butler forged the treatment links between Willmar State Hospital and Hazelden. He made Hazelden the beneficiary of the hospital's expertise. His primary focus during the fifties was rehabilitation and how to make Hazelden the best possible treatment center. He was very aware of Bradley's innovative style as well as his uncertainty about where everything would lead. Although Butler was excited about events at Willmar, he was primarily interested in Hazelden's future. He saw the great potential in linking the private, freestanding Hazelden to the discoveries of and the direction taken by Willmar. Likewise, he was anxious to link Hazelden with the research potential and educational direction of Yale. He sensed that the field was at the edge of a new frontier in helping a major group of abandoned people.

A keen observer of people, Butler soon intuited the abilities of the young Anderson. He came to believe that the psychologist, although not recovering, had the potential to span the geographical distance and the attitudinal differences between

The Bridge to Hazelden

Willmar and Center City. In the late sixties Butler, in his foresight, encouraged Anderson to initiate training programs for counselors and for clergy, not only to serve Hazelden's purposes but also to assist the field nationally and later internationally. It was Butler's vision that propelled Hazelden to assume the role of a pioneer within and outside the field of chemical dependency.

Dan Anderson departing for Russia in August 1986. Because of Anderson's talents for bridging the gap between AA and the professionals, invitations to speak came from across the world.

When Bradley told Anderson in 1960 that he had accepted a position with Lutheran General Hospital in Chicago to replicate the Willmar experience there, he asked Anderson to go with him. By this time, however, Pat Butler had been pursuing Anderson, and he was. excited about the possibilities that existed at Hazelden—at Center City, at the Fellowship Club in St. Paul, and at Dia Linn, Hazelden's treatment center for women. Butler was determined to assist alcoholics as long as science had not found a solution to the problem and alcoholics needed help. In those days many people expected science to make a breakthrough. When there wasn't any, Butler simply said let's do what we can do. Anderson found Butler's mission compelling enough to decide to take him up on his offer of employment with Hazelden.

It was a sad parting of the ways for Bradley and Anderson. Looking back on the early days, Bradley reflected: "I don't think our emotions were any grand ones. We were all able to relate to one another. It was always the same people who stuck together—all the people who came and went over a ten-year period—the same ones who talked about the same things, or talked in a similar fashion." For Anderson and Bradley the decade had been an adventure. Each would take the experience of that decade and plant, cultivate, and harvest it in a new soil and setting.

Anderson's Curiosity and Creativity

Like other professionals, Anderson initially found AA mysterious, but, unlike many professionals, Anderson's suspicions made him inquisitive—a curiosity enveloped in genuine openness. His inquisitiveness led to the insights that convinced him about the validity of AA. Like the other professionals in the Willmar adventure, Anderson had to find his way. His unique talent was his ability to translate the problem of and the solution to the disease into categories that professionals could understand.

Professionals at this time were easily intimidated when they heard the problem of alcoholism described in the Big Book and in the first three Steps as one of "powerlessness," and the solution as trust in a "Power greater than myself." When Anderson was writing the goals and purposes of Hazelden's recovery process, he noted that the model at Hazelden is one of learning to accept a chronic condition. Patients are helped to realize that this basic condition cannot be altered, so they must give up the struggle to change the fact and instead choose to concentrate on using available resources to live with it in a constructive manner. Anderson would then encourage attendance at AA by urging that identification with others who share the condition and are in the process of accomplishing this task is a key factor in the recovery process.

Anderson regarded treatment as holistic when he classified the illness as multiphasic, extending to all the dimensions of an individual—intellectual, physical, emotional, social/familial, and spiritual. As such, treatment demanded a multidisciplinary response, that is, a team of professionals that included physicians, nurses, psychologists, social workers, AA counselors, chaplains, and recreational therapists.

The changes that Anderson would introduce at Hazelden eventually gained acceptance because he was able to grasp the reasoning of the alcoholic. He also was able to develop the right kind of empathy and speak the language of the alcoholic, whether in private counseling sessions or in his lectures. Pat Butler recalled, "I remember Selden Bacon [director of the Yale Summer School of Alcohol Studies] sitting next to me while Dan lectured on the topic of 'Learning Theories,' and Bacon said, 'Where did that guy come from?' He did not expect to discover any experts at Hazelden." Anderson had the ability to bridge the gap between AA and the professionals, which he did through the classes he taught at Rutgers and on the national and international speaking circuit.

With Bradley's departure for Lutheran General in Chicago, Anderson accepted Butler's offer to become the executive director and vice president of Hazelden in October 1961. The various Hazelden campuses would now serve as his laboratory for testing his ideas on treatment. Anderson's acceptance of Butler's offer, however, was tempered with some trepidation because he was not certain how things would work out given the strong personality and entrenched position of Lynn Carroll as the director at Center City and as the personal friend and AA sponsor of Pat Butler. It was a delicate situation. Anderson was astute enough to realize that for the time being he could not establish his office at Center City. He knew that it would take some time, if ever, before he could persuade Lynn Carroll and the staff at Center City to accept and introduce his ideas. Pat Butler offered him the opportunity to work out of the Butler Office in St. Paul, but Anderson felt that would be too constrictive. He decided to locate his office at Fellowship Club in St. Paul. He needed to be where the action was—with the patients and staff developing and implementing programs. To be close to Dia Linn in Dellwood, Anderson moved his family to the neighboring community of White Bear Lake. He then fashioned Dia Linn into his "laboratory," where he could introduce, experiment with, and refine the multidisciplinary approach of Willmar.

The Founding of Dia Linn

Dia Linn, Hazelden's original treatment center for women, emerged at a time when very little was being done to help female alcoholics. Pat Butler, who chaired the Minnesota Advisory Board on the Problems of Alcoholism, believed together with this board that something had to be done to help female alcoholics. Rather than wait for the board to act, however, Butler and some other Hazelden board members decided in May 1956 to purchase a property in Dellwood—a 300-acre estate that had been the home of W. O. Washburn, a St. Paul industrialist. Butler, upon returning from a trip to Ireland, christened the estate Dia Linn, Gaelic for "God be with us." In addition to the main manor, there was a small guest cottage and two other cottages, all in excellent condition and ready for year-round occupancy. The setting and facilities provided an ideal environment for the treatment of alcoholism. Comfortable surroundings, an understanding staff, and association with others with a similar problem—all combined to cultivate within the women who came for treatment a sense of hope and purposeful living without the crutch of alcohol and other drugs.

The women at Dia Linn were already familiar with Anderson. Starting in 1957 the patients had been traveling to Center City every other Saturday to hear Anderson's lectures. In 1960, at Anderson's suggestion and directed by Pat Butler, members of the Dia Linn staff went to Willmar to observe the alcoholism treatment program there. Conversely, some of the staff at Willmar came to Dia Linn to observe and suggest changes. In July 1962, Anderson hired John Harkness, a clinical psychologist, as director of Dia Linn. Through Harkness, Anderson was able to introduce a more structured and professional approach to the treatment program with minimal resistance and hard feelings, something he knew that he could not do for the time being at Center City. At Dia Linn, working with Harkness, Anderson was able to translate and expand upon the simple treatment modalities already in place at Willmar. He introduced structure, schedule, and the sinews of consistency in the program that became his experimental laboratory. What was tried, tested, and found to be valid and workable was later introduced in the Center City program.

A multidisciplinary staff was forged, although all the functions were not yet clearly defined, and formal charting procedures were established with the use of intake forms and counselor and nursing notes (in stark contrast to the use of index cards that would remain the method at Center City until 1965). Patients were assigned to specific counselors, group therapy sessions became the norm, and a daily schedule was put in place. At staff meetings every morning, patients would be discussed and files would be read and added to. Three educational lectures every day became the staple of the program, one each in the morning, afternoon, and evening. That was something that was sacred to Anderson. Every Friday afternoon and evening, aftercare sessions were held, which brought alumni and their spouses from local and distant places. Some Fridays there were as many as fifty returning Dia Linn pilgrims eager to share their newly discovered fellowship and sobriety.

The structural and therapeutic changes introduced at Dia Linn did not radically alter the program as it existed in its pristine form in Center City. They were made to improve patient care. Nonetheless, there were tensions at Dellwood between the old and the new, the cherished and the changed, the unstructured and the structured, the strict AA approach of the recovering counselor and the modified AA approach of the professional. These tensions foreshadowed the much more serious strained relations and ultimate rift between Lynn Carroll and Dan Anderson, between whom Pat Butler would eventually have to choose.

5
Changes at Center City

When Dan Anderson spoke, people listened. Pictured above at right, Dan speaks at Hazelden's twenty-fifth anniversary celebration, at (middle photo) the 1987 retiree celebration, and (bottom) at the groundbreaking ceremony for the Renewal Center.

In the meantime, the patient population at Center City had doubled the six years prior to 1964. Anderson explained to the board that the lack of space prevented the delivery of adequate services: "[Hazelden has] inadequate nursing personnel, inadequate fully trained staff, the need to transfer patients to St. Croix hospital when immediate detoxification is required (instead of being licensed to do it on campus); the need for daily rounds of patients; lack of lavatory facilities; lack of counseling areas; inadequate facilities for food preparation; the disturbing effect of overcrowding on patient therapy." The board heard the message. Nonetheless, expanding was a decision over which many of the board members agonized. Bringing the men and women together on the Center City campus did not set well with some of the board members, staff, and alumni. Back in 1956, before the Dellwood property had been chosen for Dia Linn, Lynn Carroll had refused to set aside a few acres of isolated land for a women's unit at Center City, saying, "They don't make bear traps big enough to keep them [men and women] apart."

Another devilish issue lurking in the minds of most of

the board was the "what if" scorpions so prevalent in nonalcoholic as well as alcoholic thinking: What if Hazelden doubled or even tripled its capacity and no one were to come? What if the program were modified in such a way that it were no longer effective? Whatever it was at the Old Lodge—the small size, the familiarity, the intimacy, the freedom, the simplicity—it worked. People came, people were restored, people departed, people recovered—it was a simple enough formula. Would institutionalizing Hazelden by constructing new buildings destroy the formula? Numbers and effectiveness—was there a correlation? During all of his association with Hazelden, Anderson continually wrestled with the census. He couldn't let go of it, for ultimately he looked upon himself as responsible for filling the beds upon which Hazelden's present and future depended.

Pat Butler, his wife, Aimee, and Dan Anderson were the three people primarily engaged with the architects in designing the new Hazelden complex. Anderson in particular felt the need to structure the buildings in such a way that they would capture the strengths of the Old Lodge while allowing for the implementation of his program design. The architects were continually reminded that the success of the program was in its small numbers and casual atmosphere. The architects' solution was to provide a small and intimate unit atmosphere limited to groups of between

Hazelden's treatment units were built based in part on Dan Anderson's vision of a group of buildings that would capture the strengths of the Old Lodge while allowing for the implementation of the Minnesota Model of treatment.

Hazelden's modern treatment units

eighteen and twenty-two patients, while at the same time making the individual part of the larger community of Hazelden during lectures and meals. What they created was an extraordinary piece of architecture that preserved individuality while promoting congeniality and camaraderie. The new rehabilitation units graced its inhabitants with dignity, proving once and for all that a quality environment could be created and maintained for the treatment of the alcoholic.

The years from 1964 to 1966 were particularly demanding from the point of view of personal transition and change for both Anderson and Lynn Carroll. Carroll had carefully nurtured the treatment program that he had put in place in 1949. Nonetheless, Hazelden now belonged to another generation. These years witnessed the changing of the guard—old departures and new arrivals.

Until January 1964, Anderson's office was located at Fellowship Club. Although he was Hazelden's vice president and executive director, responsible for the total operation of Hazelden, he supervised Center City from a distance. Lynn Carroll, on the other hand, directed the treatment program at the Old Lodge in Center City, and Anderson was reluctant to intrude into the old master's kingdom. With the decision to expand, Anderson had to abandon his reluctance and take the direction of Center City firmly in hand. He relocated his family to Taylors

Falls and his office to Center City. The tension between Anderson and Carroll had been inevitable but bearable as long as the two did not encounter one another frequently and as long as Carroll commandeered the Old Lodge. But soon the Old Lodge would be just another one of many units on the campus. Lon Jacobson, a longtime friend and assistant to Lynn Carroll, said that the ultimate reason for Carroll's eventual departure was "the encroachment of the downtown office [meaning Pat Butler and Dan Anderson] on the running of Hazelden."

Anderson chaired the staff meetings at Center City in preparation for the new programs and the new buildings. Carroll attended initially but his participation was perfunctory and gradually diminished to absenteeism. Beginning in January 1965, Anderson began to hire a variety of professionals to help implement the multidisciplinary model. The first of these was the Reverend Gordon Grimm, who would represent and manage in subsequent years the pastoral and training dimensions of the developing Hazelden continuum. He became Anderson's closest associate and confidant. This was followed shortly by the hiring of Eugene Wojtowicz, a psychologist and a capable consultant in personnel matters. As Anderson tapped into Wojtowicz's organizational skills, Wojtowicz assumed greater control over Hazelden in a way that caused concern among many staff members.

The Reverend Gordon Grimm (facing camera), the chief architect of Hazelden's pastoral and training programs. He became Anderson's closest associate and confidant.

Wojtowicz's addition to the staff signaled the psychologists' entrenchment on the Center City campus and was deeply resented by Lynn Carroll, who up until that time had resisted the residency of any psychologist. Carroll feared that the mere presence of the psychologist in the treatment process meant that many people would misinterpret the nature of the illness of alcoholism as primarily a psychological one. Preserving the delicate balance between understanding alcoholism as a primary chronic illness and allowing the psychologist to have a prominent role on the multidisciplinary team was not an easy one then or even today.

But it was not just those outside his field of psychology whom Anderson needed to educate. He encountered other psychologists who either considered the alcoholic a lost cause or who held to the belief that alcoholism was a symptom of some other personality disorder. In either case, Anderson's ideas were suspect. Reflecting on those times, he recalled, "In the early days of alcoholism [treatment], I was considered an inferior professional working with alcoholics—and was looked down upon."

Besides being viewed as a second-class citizen in his own field of psychology, he also had to work through the relationship with the counselors who, as recovering alcoholics, were innately suspicious of the psychologists. Among all the professionals who composed the multidisciplinary team it was the psychologist of whom the counselor was most wary. At Willmar it was relatively easy since the professionals were entrenched there first and the counselors had to tread carefully to establish their credentials. But it was different at Hazelden where the recovering counselors were entrenched, in command, and openly hostile. Lon Jacobson, one of the treatment counselors, threatened Wojtowicz when he pulled a patient from a lecture to give him the results of an MMPI. It took awhile for the psychologists to gain acceptance, but the staffing pattern that Anderson envisioned dictated their presence. During the subsequent years of Hazelden's history there was a constant tug-of-war for the controlling role in the treatment of the patients.

Another way of looking at the differences between professionals and counselors was in their views of the relationship between chemical dependency and mental health. There were a number of evolving treatment views of this relationship. Initially, before the Willmar experience, psychiatry looked upon alcoholism as merely a symptom of a mental health problem. Then, as the chemical dependency field and treatment counselors gathered strength, the appearance of mental health symptoms were regarded as transient manifestations of alcoholism that would disappear with the arrest of the illness of chemical dependency. By the late seventies, however, it was recognized that the "crazy behavior" did not always disappear when the patient began to recover from chemical dependency through an abstinence program.

Anderson encouraged the multidisciplinary staff to recognize and come to grips with the existence of dual illnesses—both chemical dependency and a mental disorder—that some of the patients were beginning to exhibit. These patients with dual disorders required services for both problems, and Anderson wanted the staff to treat the whole person. The dual-disorder patients would begin to appear with increasing frequency in the eighties and nineties, and only in the latter decade did Hazelden begin to deal with these patients more openly and directly. But from 1965 to 1975 Anderson had to arbitrate between the two, and he did this by balancing the composition of the staff.

Anderson had a tough choice to make in selecting the leader of the Center City rehabilitation program. In 1966 he appointed Dick Solberg, a recovering person who was on the staff at Dia Linn, to be the chief counselor at Center City, responsible for the program there. The decision deeply disappointed John Harkness, the psychologist who had expected to be director of Rehabilitation Services. But it was a clever and wise move on the part of Anderson, who did not want to antagonize Carroll and his supporters any further by putting a psychologist in charge of treatment. Anderson's mandate was clear: Solberg was to hire the counseling staff who would represent the core element of the multidisciplinary team for the four new units under construction. Anderson suggested two criteria: (1) that counselors be recovering and in AA, and (2) that they be good speakers. For the remainder of the professional team Anderson would draw heavily on people who had been associated with Willmar State Hospital.

Disillusioned by what he considered the triumph of the MMPI and the reading of the tea leaves, Carroll participated less and less in the changes that were occurring. He felt alone and abandoned, especially when Jacobson departed in 1965. Carroll's role at the Old Lodge was limited to weekends, and even then he was frequently absent. His sense of loss was great, and by the middle of 1966 it was time for him to leave—not as gracefully as he might have desired.

In the early years of the tension between Carroll and Anderson, Anderson was not sure his decisions would be supported by Pat Butler if Carroll objected to them. But Carroll said little as Anderson settled in. Finally, Butler decided that Carroll, because of his negative behavior and the influence that it was having on others both within and outside of Hazelden, would have to go. It was a painful decision for Butler because Carroll had been his AA sponsor. Carroll's departure drew attention to a serious crisis

Lynn Carroll

for Hazelden. Many of his disciples became disillusioned at what they considered the betrayal of Carroll and the abandonment of AA principles on behalf of psychology. Carroll had a great following. In the midst of the expansion, no one could ignore the serious question: Would Carroll's departure influence those Hazelden alumni who had benefited from his treatment methodology to transfer their allegiance and refer patients elsewhere? Fortunately, and to Butler's and Anderson's great relief, it did not.

One only had to listen to the lectures of the two men—Carroll and Anderson—to perceive the differences between them. Carroll was charismatic, while Anderson was intellectual—a conceptualist, although not totally dispassionate. They were not, however, totally in opposition to one another. At Center City, Carroll had provided the foundation upon which Anderson could build. After more than fifteen years of operation, Hazelden had a rehabilitation process based substantially upon AA, set in a dignified, warm, human, and personally enriching environment. Anderson was melding that program with his own tradition and imagination, again based substantially upon AA, but systematically and structurally delivered through a multidisciplinary model. Of course, there were major and minor differences, depending upon the viewpoint of the old or the new guard. The old guard saw them as major. As a consequence, it was time for a changing of the guard.

6
Evolution of the Multidisciplinary Team

Dan Anderson at a Hazelden board meeting. Along with Pat Butler, Anderson was instrumental in convincing the board to broaden Hazelden's mission statement in 1984 to include other addictions as well as health promotion.

Under Anderson's leadership and supported by the Butler family, the period from 1966 to 1975 was one of the most exciting decades in Hazelden's history. It was a time of amazing vitality and creativity, marked by a relentless flow of ideas and experimentation. The events that occurred during these ten years were guided by a group of dedicated, strong-willed individuals, diverse in tradition, character, and personality, who molded Hazelden for years to come. Among other things the decade witnessed

1. the solidification of a clearly defined treatment program with a multidisciplinary approach
2. the creation of a short-lived repeaters (relapse) program called the Golden Slippers, which became the model for other relapse programs around the country
3. the establishment of an extended care program on the new Jellinek unit
4. the emergence of a research and evaluation department and a variety of training programs, for which Hazelden became world famous
5. the tradition of family conferences, from which the Family Program evolved in 1972

6. signals from the literature department in the early seventies that its own growth would soon be explosive

These were exciting and difficult years for Anderson personally. He was able to orchestrate all the programs—treatment as well as training—according to his own experience at Willmar but blended with his ever-evolving creativity. He took the multidisciplinary concept far beyond its rudimentary stages at Willmar. The rehabilitation programs essentially revolved around an education process (the lectures), the fellowship on the units, and therapeutic engagement, which included both formal one-on-ones and group counseling. As the years progressed, the group counseling assumed a variety of forms on the different units.

Anderson had not formulated any specific job descriptions for the professionals who made up the multidisciplinary staff. He was excited about finding the right match of people, pooling their background, professional training, and personal talents, then getting them to work together as a team. Anderson allowed multidisciplinary staff to be creative about what they could do for the patients and to define their own boundaries and contributions—in essence designing their own job descriptions. Anderson emphasized the participation of the clergy on the team because of his own personal belief in the spiritual dimension of the program. Indeed, the clergy for their part fell in love with the program because they saw and felt it to be deeply spiritual and because it placed them on the same plane as the other professionals rather than in the secondary roles they experienced in other institutional settings.

But Anderson was an idealist. As time went on he became a little disappointed with all the professionals, because, while there were so many things that they could have done, the formal job descriptions that were emerging tended to cement them to those tasks that they had initially designed for themselves. Just as Hazelden was moving from a pioneering, dynamic, caring community of patients and staff to a highly structured, regulated, and institutionalized treatment center, so were the professionals losing their sense of urgency to be innovative in the treatment of patients. The straitjacket of a twenty-eight-day treatment model, to which the staff was manacled with assigned tasks and specified responsibilities, left Hazelden unprepared for the later onslaught of managed care in the eighties. Success was a problem, for it spoiled the staff and locked them into rigid roles with mechanical contributions. Anderson later lamented that this very success delayed for a long time the team's willingness and ability to transfer their knowledge and technology into other areas such as a variety of chronic lifestyle disorders.

The Shackles of a Twenty-Eight-Day Program

When Minnesota mandated twenty-eight days of insurance coverage in the early seventies, it was viewed as a real blessing for many people who would otherwise not receive treatment. It took time to overcome a patient's denial, to initiate behavioral changes, and to procure a commitment to a radically altered lifestyle, and the twenty-day-treatment model had been clinically tested and experientially proven by the passage of years. The mandate, however, encouraged staff to stick with a twenty-eight-day plan. In this way, the mandate could be viewed as a curse, for it brought about a complacency among those who practiced the Minnesota Model. Treatment plans began to replicate one another around four weeks of treatment, stifling the creativity that the Minnesota Model had shown up to that point. Clinicians knew how to add to the program and increase the length of stay; they knew how to add to the program without increasing the length of stay; but they simply did not know how to decrease the length of stay.

As the years progressed, the name Hazelden came to be identified with a twenty-eight-day treatment program, when in reality the name ought to have conjured up a whole continuum of imaginative services that emerged at Hazelden and throughout Minnesota over the course of many years.

Managed Care

Insurance companies had never been pleased with Minnesota's early seventies mandate that all insurance policies carry a minimum of twenty-eight days of residential treatment for chemical dependency. In the early eighties, treatment providers had gotten a bad name as hospital administrators were desperately looking for ways to fill their vacant beds. The insurance-covered chemical dependency industry appeared especially lucrative. At the same time, treatment centers and clinics proliferated and the fierce competition to maintain a high census was exacerbated by unprofessional tactics in filling those beds. Addictions multiplied; anyone rumored to be addicted was a likely candidate for treatment. Some referrals were overdiagnosed or misdiagnosed.

Into this climate stepped managed care. By the mid-eighties the insurance companies had managed to bypass mandated coverage by insisting that the patient demonstrate medical necessity. The criteria for medical necessity were determined by the managed care company, which made them so stringent and narrow that only a small percentage could qualify. Furthermore, Hazelden began losing contracts with companies to provide treatment services through employee assistance programs. Managed care could offer services at a lower cost. Many of the companies with which Hazelden had a long-standing relationship began opting to have managed care companies run their employee health care plans.

Success also prevented Hazelden from exploring the dual disorders of some patients and moving realistically into the treatment of the whole person. A multidisciplinary staff could have done this very easily, for the professional skills and talent were available. But the concentration on problems just associated with chemical dependency blinded staff to the need to deal with other, unrelated disorders. Anderson urged, cajoled, and exhorted the pursuit of these important arenas by the staff. Together with Pat Butler, Anderson supported a change in Hazelden's mission statement that would allow this expansion. After much agonizing and not without resistance from some, the board revised the mission statement in 1984 to expand into the areas of other addictions as well as prevention and health promotion. Although Educational Materials quickly seized the opportunity to publish in these areas, the Rehabilitation Division and its multidisciplinary staff did not avail itself of the change. While the success of Anderson's attempts to move in broader directions was limited at the time, the implementation of these ideas did finally occur after his retirement, when the board once again in 1998 reiterated its desire that Hazelden expand in these directions and approved a reorganization that would facilitate such an expansion.

7
Challenges at Hazelden

There is much metaphorical significance that Dan Anderson's "other" labor of love throughout his career was sailing—charting new courses, braving strong weather, and enjoying the fruits that only a willingness to take risks can bear.

Amid the evolution of the Minnesota Model, Anderson also faced nitty-gritty administrative issues that consumed enormous amounts of his time, dampened his enthusiasm, and put weighty constraints on his public speaking and off-campus activities. Obtaining the skilled nursing home license for the new Ignatia Hall required putting into writing the nursing standards as well as the detoxification protocols, most of which fell upon Anderson. He also headed up a one-person personnel department charged with the task of developing job descriptions and compensation guidelines. He was responsible for written policies and procedures to meet the criteria and standards of the newly formulated state licensure rules. Then the Joint Commission on the Accreditation of Hospitals established another set of standards that had to be met for chemical dependency treatment. Anderson did not like the world of rules and regulations in which he had to be politically correct. He managed, however, to temper his rebellious nature as he grew older. His attitude toward the business world was much the same, and he had to hold his tongue when board decisions hinged on the bottom line rather than on whether a program would help the needy.

At the same time that he was engaged in the details of administrative and managerial activities, Anderson also felt that it was important for him to be out on the road, speaking, educating, and training others about this new model of recovery and the great benefits that it held for society. He knew that the public had to be educated if the treatment of alcoholism were to be accepted. He became, without a doubt and without a peer, Hazelden's best spokesperson.

Butler tolerated Anderson's being on the road for a time. He agreed that if the Hazelden model were to succeed, the public—both professional and nonprofessional—would have to be educated. But Butler also felt very strongly that someone had to mind the store. He became particularly disturbed in 1971 when Grimm, in addition to Anderson, began teaching at the Rutgers Summer School of Alcohol Studies for three weeks every year. Butler was worried that Hazelden patients would be neglected. There was another issue also—Hazelden was still not paying its way, and Butler was tired of making up the annual shortfall out of his own pocket.

These issues so disturbed Butler that in 1971 he was seriously thinking of resigning as president of Hazelden. When Anderson's assistant, Eugene Wojtowicz, who was also secretary to the board, suggested to Butler that he replace Anderson as director, Butler immediately put down the palace coup and sent Wojtowicz packing to Edgewood, a treatment facility in St. Louis. Butler's loyalty to Anderson precluded any change in leadership; Wojtowicz had overplayed his hand.

Before acting on his threat to resign, Butler was prevailed upon to call in some consultants who would help respond to his concerns. As a result of this outside input, Hazelden was reorganized in such a way that Butler became the chairman of the board, and Anderson became the president of Hazelden with only two direct reports—from the directors of Rehabilitation and Administrative Services. A few years later Anderson's responsibility for internal management was eased even further when Harold Swift (a social worker hired in 1966 to specialize in family problems relating to alcohol) was appointed the administrator, reporting to Anderson but principally responsible for the administrative and internal functions of Hazelden. Butler's specific charge to Swift was to pay attention to detail and to balance the budget. Anderson was now free to be out on the road, exchanging ideas, sharing what Hazelden was doing. He was not shy about giving to others. It was only in giving that one would receive. Many people throughout the world are grateful to Anderson for his generosity.

What many people did not know was that during the decade from 1966 to 1975, which demanded so much of

Anderson's energy, both at work and helping to raise a large family of ten children, he was suffering terribly from kidney stones. He had been to the doctor but was unable to pass the stones. He went to Mayo Clinic for major surgery, but the kidney stones reappeared. Since then he underwent two more surgeries, but each time the stones reappeared. Oftentimes his condition was so painful that Marie would have to find babysitters at the last minute in order to drive Dan to gatherings where he was the principal speaker. He hardly ever missed a commitment no matter how ill he was feeling. When the presentation was over he would return to where Marie was waiting, white as a sheet, and she would drive home with Dan getting as comfortable as he could in the backseat of the car. Eventually, the stones stopped bothering him, even though he was never able to rid himself of them.

Anderson had his own planning method long before strategic planning became the vogue at Hazelden. It was often described as the grazing philosophy, which allowed Hazelden to seize opportunities by responding wherever there was a pressing need. Anderson moved principally toward the needs of the underserved populations—young people, women, inhabitants of rural areas, and senior citizens. Through Anderson, Hazelden made a serious and successful effort to assist the Native American population, especially through the Training and the Continuing

Education departments. Because Anderson had long been concerned about mixing young people with the older population at Center City, he convinced the board in 1981 to buy New Pioneer House in Plymouth, Minnesota, which eventually became the very successful Hazelden Center for Youth and Families. At the risk of being called an empire builder, Anderson prevailed upon the board to establish Hazelden's first major venture outside the state of Minnesota at the invitation of Mr. and Mrs. Jack Hanley. Despite some critical years, the Hanley-Hazelden Center, a rehabilitation facility in West Palm Beach, Florida, eventually became a renowned center of excellence for senior citizens. Mr. Hanley described Anderson as the "wise old owl."

That same wise old owl, never at risk of becoming an endangered species, pushed the board to sponsor both the Renewal Center for the benefit of the recovery community and the Cork Center to focus on the areas of prevention and health promotion. During the eighties, both before and after his retirement in 1986, Anderson was convinced that prevention was the best solution to the problem of chemical dependency. Indirectly, prevention has always been a part of Hazelden's mission. Educational Materials (Publishing) had been entrusted with that task, informally before it became a division and more formally after 1975. It published a variety of items seeking to educate the public, professionals, and families about alcoholism, its early warning signs and early intervention.

But Anderson, always cognizant of Hazelden's hesitation, even reluctance, to cross the gulf between treatment and prevention, had encouraged more direct approaches. One of these was to penetrate the country's educational system at every level to educate teachers and students about alcohol abuse and its consequences. With the building of the Cork Center, Anderson found an ally in its benefactor Joan Kroc in promoting the cause of prevention, which became part of larger umbrella, first called wellness and then health promotion. This outreach effort embraced a wide variety of programs promoting healthy lifestyles, vocational changes, and prevention in schools. Anderson believed that Hazelden's future goal was to help improve the lifestyle of anyone who came in contact with Hazelden—not only to prevent chronic diseases, including chemical dependency, but also to teach people of all ages to change their lives in positive ways. A decade after his retirement, Hazelden's evolving mission included Anderson's vision.

In 1982, Anderson announced to the board that he would retire from the presidency when he reached the age of sixty-five in 1986. In order to prepare for his departure in an appropriate fashion, as well as to review the status of Hazelden, the board of trustees hired Richard M. Byrd to conduct a management audit, called the Byrd Report, and to provide recommendations for an orderly succession. Completed in 1983, the Byrd Report provided a succession plan that was highly critical of the heir apparent, Harold Swift, and suggested a reorganization that returned to Anderson certain administrative duties of which he had been relieved in 1971. Pat Butler, still chairman of the board, was unhappy with the reorganization plan. And Byrd was chagrined because Anderson would not bring the board's attention to Swift's deficiencies. For his part, Swift was unhappy with Byrd because of the manner in which the management audit was conducted. The success of the Byrd Report could probably be measured by the fact that no one was happy with it. Nonetheless, the report put its finger on some serious issues.

The audit also indicated certain areas in which Swift should be trained in order to be considered as Anderson's successor. This task was made awkward as the board took upon itself part of the training process, consultants were hired to help Swift in other areas, and Anderson was required to oversee the cultivation of Swift's planning and organizational abilities, especially in mapping out succession plans for each of Hazelden's divisions. Moreover, the board requested that Anderson meet with Swift on a regular basis to try to improve his public relations "persona." It was not an easy time for either Anderson or Swift. The two had had a fairly good relationship up to this time, but it deteriorated during the transition, which was unnecessarily long.

Swift and Anderson worked very well as the inside-outside men, even though they had different styles and personalities. Swift was a soft-spoken, unassuming, easygoing individual who went about his job without a lot of fanfare. While he possessed a dry and subtle humor, he appeared awkward, reticent, nervous, and even shy in public. Anderson, on the other hand, was propelled by nervous energy and did not like to sit long in one spot. Consequently, he could be seen at almost any place on the Hazelden campus discussing problems and theories with patients and staff. Visiting alumni were constantly seeking him out for advice on any number of issues. Anderson was always available. He was a generalist and Swift was a detail man. Swift liked working with standards and licensure regulations, while Anderson was more concerned with the quality of treatment that derived from the concept and practice of the caring community. Swift was budget conscious, while Anderson felt that certain non-revenue-producing departments such as training and prevention were worth their weight in gold for the goodwill they spread throughout the United States and the world. Swift was lukewarm about Hazelden's prevention efforts.

Swift threatened to resign if the organizational structure suggested by the Byrd Report was implemented.

Fortunately for Swift, Pat Butler concurred with him. On the other hand, Swift agreed to follow the recommendations of the board to improve his managerial style in the areas suggested by the report—team building, communication with and among the directors, and strategic planning. A number of consultants were brought in to help Swift in his leadership style and development.

The succession issue raised by the Byrd Report reminded Anderson of the occasion when, during another management audit, he asked the consultant what he was most surprised about. The consultant replied that he was looking for but could not find the young turks who would be responsible for and inspire the future of Hazelden. He found that the fire was still in the bellies of Anderson and Butler, and he was unable to find the visionaries who would replace them. It was on that occasion, later confirmed many times over, that Anderson began to realize Hazelden's failure to develop succession plans and people with passion and creativity. The Byrd Report not only highlighted this issue when it came to Anderson's successor but also pointed out that no one had been concerned about the development of personnel to fill key roles, and in general the organization did not pay attention to divisional human resource issues.

Nonetheless, Anderson had to prepare for his departure from Hazelden, which was formally announced in the spring of 1985, effective March 31, 1986. What everyone was concerned about was that Anderson should not leave Hazelden precipitously. Such a move would not be good either for Anderson personally or for the organization, as it would appear to signify the abandonment of Hazelden. The plan was for Anderson to cut back gradually upon his work during the next year and a half, but in such a way that his gradual relinquishment of tasks would go unnoticed. This was difficult for Anderson to do, given his penchant for work as well as the demand for his wisdom and talents. But he did it gracefully, with charm and with wit. The emphasis at his retirement party was on the transitional role that Anderson would play in the future at Hazelden as president emeritus in charge of development. In the planning for the party and in the news releases, everyone was instructed to be very careful not to give the impression that Anderson was moving out and on to other things.

As president emeritus, Anderson continued to labor in Hazelden's vineyard as a member of the board of trustees, urging the board to support the area of prevention and to become more active in providing leadership and strategic planning. Under Pat Butler, the board had assumed a mostly passive role. Anderson was deeply concerned about trivializing the concept of addiction. If every bad habit was an addiction, then nothing was an addiction.

On behalf of Hazelden and the Development Office, Anderson continued to assume speaking engagements throughout the United States to alumni and to the public in general. Pat Butler often referred to Anderson as Hazelden's Hubert Humphrey because of his ability to communicate on and off the cuff.

8
Reflections on the Past, Present, and Future

Dan and Marie

※━◎━※

In the early nineties, Anderson had to slow down because of a heart condition. As he moved further away from Hazelden and active participation in its affairs, he often reminisced about the chemical dependency field, its strengths and weaknesses, and his own regrets as well as his satisfaction and sense of fulfillment. He was especially anxious about the professionals in the field. He could not hide his disappointment that most of the professional staff at Hazelden got frozen into structured roles, locked into a certain way of doing things. Success had spoiled them and prevented them from transferring their knowledge and methodology into other areas of chronic illness, addictive behaviors, and dual disabilities.

As he reflected upon the past, present, and future of Hazelden, Anderson believed that its very existence as well as its success depended upon matching the ever-evolving patient profile not only with staff professionalism and competence but also with flexibility and creativity. More than anyone else, Anderson knew that the contemporary alcohol and drug abuse clients looked very different than those patients of two, or even one decade ago. Besides having multiple drug problems, they were now presenting themselves at Hazelden's doors with multiple mental, emotional, and physical problems, some related, some unrelated to their chemical dependency. He believed that Hazelden's counselors of the future would need to have not only knowledge and counseling skills for chemical dependency but also more educational degrees with specialized knowledge and skills in other areas.

Anderson saw clearly that Hazelden's success during the sixties and seventies could be a barrier to keeping up with the changes and advances that others were suggesting. The specter of change was frightening. Hazelden became obsessed with filling beds as the mark of success. Anderson was concerned that Hazelden increasingly measured value in terms of the bottom line, and not, as it did in its early and middle years, in terms of patient care for the unfortunate and the underserved and in terms of the goodwill that spilled over into the community. He considered suffering some losses or merely breaking even as being part of Hazelden's mission. He was a warrior and prophet continuously weighing in against the commercialization of the whole recovery movement, admonishing against Hazelden's commercialization of compassion and its institutionalization of the caring community. The closing down of the Clinical Pastoral Education Program in 1992 caused him great concern and pain. He felt it to be a pragmatic action that lost sight of the historical value of the program and the tremendous contribution it had made to the community.

As he looked back over the history of the efforts to respond to the national problem of chemical dependency during the past fifty years, of which he had been an integral part, Anderson found reinforcement for the axiom that history repeats itself. Paradoxically, despite all the progress that had been made, it seemed as though the field was right back where it had started. Anderson felt an eerie déjà-vu quality about the present. In the old days he and his colleagues had gone about telling the world that alcoholism was an identifiable illness, that alcoholics needed help and were worth helping. Now all the old barriers have been resurrected: the renewed conflict over the disease concept, the return of the stigma, the prisons with their revolving doors, the massive cultural hostility and intolerance. As he looked to the future, it was clear to Anderson that a new set of prophets would have to emerge to follow in the footsteps of the Andersons, the Bradleys, and the Butlers to re-educate and reinspire a variety of audiences.

Anderson was especially fond of training the counselors and clergy at Hazelden as well as lecturing weekly to the patients. His lectures were both educational and entertaining, spiced with a wry humor that became Anderson's hallmark. Rarely did his listeners lose interest. He took special care of the lecture series at Hazelden, designing the format and the content. He felt that this educational process allowed the patients to sit in the lecture hall in an anonymous fashion initially reflecting on how the contents applied to others on the unit and finally at some point recognizing that what was being said applied to them also.

Anderson's educational efforts included participation on local, state, and national committees. His experience, knowledge, wisdom, and willingness to share with his colleagues won him many friends, few (if any) enemies, and the gratitude of those he helped. He took great pride in teaching first at Yale and then at Rutgers in the summer. In those very early years in the sixties, the composition of the class included those who knew it all and those who thought they knew it all. But most came because in reality they knew nothing about the subject and went away satisfied that something could be said on behalf of alcoholism as an illness and the possibilities of treating it. Anderson never knew what to expect in a class, which included psychiatrists, psychologists, and other professionals as well as recovering alcoholics. Sometimes the discussions were heated. People came from all over the country to attend one of the few schools that offered classes on the subject and research of alcoholism.

Throughout his professional career Anderson, first at Willmar and then at Hazelden, had been an advocate of research and evaluation into the effectiveness of treatment. At Willmar he and a colleague named Joseph Lucero had compiled an evaluation paper as early as 1956. In 1970 Anderson implemented a comprehensive study to determine the effectiveness of Hazelden's treatment program, measured in terms of how people functioned following treatment. Hazelden was a pioneer in this research. But, as with so many other things, people were slow to change the evaluation tool, and by the early eighties Anderson was disappointed that staff had resisted modification of the methodology and approach. But after his retirement his admonitions were heeded when Hazelden began in 1995 to chart a new course for its research department.

While not a prolific writer (he did not enjoy writing), Anderson and his colleagues co-wrote papers on research and evaluation that were important contributions to the field when they appeared because they demonstrated Hazelden's willingness and seriousness in validating the results of chemical dependency treatment. Three of his works remain classics in the field: (1) *Perspectives on Treatment: The Minnesota Experience* (1981), (2) *The Psychopathology of Denial* (1984), and (3) *Living with a Chronic Illness* (1986).

Though a humble man, Anderson is particularly proud of the support he provided and received from the AA community. Although initially skeptical of the AA program and philosophy, principally because he knew nothing about it, he soon came to understand that it was a powerful agent for keeping alcoholics sober. He embraced the movement wholeheartedly and supported M. Scott Peck's evaluation that it was one of the most significant movements of the twentieth century. AA members throughout the United States came to love and trust Anderson. He was constantly commenting upon the spirituality of the Twelve Steps and the illness. By invitation he was a friend of AA cofounder Bill W. He likes to recount that he learned more about the meaning of the Lord's Prayer from two AA members than he did anywhere else, for they practiced and lived its contents.

As this volume goes to press, Anderson continues to age gracefully and with quiet dignity. He reads voraciously (*The New Yorker* is still part of his daily fare), watches over his garden with tender loving care, takes long walks conscientiously, surrenders to his love of travel especially during the long Minnesota winters, and spends his most valued time with Marie and his children: Dennis (age 44), Patricia (43), Colleen (42), David (41), Cheryl (40), Douglas (39), Dean (37), Cynthia (36), Corrine (32), and Monica (28).

On top of everything else, Dan gives an occasional presentation at Hazelden, and with fond and faithful memories reminisces about Hazelden's legacy.

Paraphrasing John Henry Cardinal Newman:

> *Therein lies the nobility of the man—*
> *that he had the courage*
> *to dare something.*

Bibliography

The following sources were used for this biographical sketch of Dan Anderson:
- The Anderson collection, containing papers and files on a variety of subjects, located at Center City.
- Interviews conducted by the author with Dan and Marie Anderson.
- Other interviews conducted by the author with friends and Hazelden colleagues of Dan Anderson.
- McElrath, Damian, *Hazelden—A Spiritual Odyssey*. Center City, Minn.: Hazelden Foundation, 1987. (The Author has relied on this work in narrating Anderson's relationship with Hazelden.)
- McElrath, Damian, *Further Reflections on Hazelden's Spiritual Odyssey*. Center City, Minn.: Hazelden Foundation, 1998.

Publications at the back of this book:
- *The Psychopathology of Denial,* and *Behavioral Management of Chronic Illness* (formerly titled *Living with a Chronic Illness*).

Bibliography

As Hazelden begins to provide services for chronic illnesses beyond chemical dependency, the Hazelden Pittman Archives decided to reprint two excerpts of Dr. Anderson's. While the references and bibliography have not been updated, the chronic illness volume demonstrates Dr. Anderson's prescience for the field of chronic illness, which until recently was noticeably neglected. The volume also serves as a cornerstone of principles and knowledge upon which Hazelden has already begun to build.

Appendixes: Dan Anderson's Selected Essays

THE PSYCHOPATHOLOGY OF DENIAL

by

Daniel J. Anderson, Ph.D.

© Hazelden Foundation. A paper presented at the "Alcoholism: A Major Challenge for the 80s" seminar; Eisenhower Medical Center, Rancho Mirage, California, February 16, 1981.

Introduction

The denial of alcoholism in our culture is so ubiquitous, so all-pervasive, that it is almost impossible to comprehend its extensiveness and resistance to change.

Our societal attitudes are characterized by several pathological types of denial. We refuse to admit the extent of alcoholism as a major national health problem. We refuse to admit our profound ambivalence about drinking, especially excessive drinking. We remain blind to the existence of alcoholism in family, friends, and even ourselves until it has reached such an advanced stage that it no longer can be denied—and still we struggle to deny it. What is the matter with us?

When one looks at our history, at our confused cultural attitudes, at the moral stigma associated with alcoholism, the cultural context of denial is not hard to comprehend.[1,2] It should not surprise us then, that for the alcoholic, denial is one of the major barriers to treatment and recovery.

The focus of this pamphlet will be on the origins of denial as it is imbedded in the larger frame of reference known as the mechanisms of defense. Following a review of the major defense mechanisms, the psychopathology of denial in alcoholism will be discussed as this is seen in the alcoholic, the family, and the community.

Finally, an attempt will be made to illustrate the methods of dealing with denial in formal alcoholism treatment programs.

The pervasiveness of denial in alcoholics, even after successful treatment, will also be pointed out as one of the major reasons for the value of Alcoholics Anonymous and Al-Anon as ongoing health maintenance programs.

Appendix 1

The Mechanisms of Defense

Self-esteem seems to come built into human nature. All of us want to regard ourselves as worthy. We also very much want to have others regard and appraise us as worthy, effective, valuable human beings. It could well be that psychological well-being or mental health is directly related to maintaining—at almost any cost—our sense of self-esteem. Thus, this primary concern about self-worth may be our major psychological concern in life following the need for food, clothing, and shelter. William McDougall called it "the master sentiment of self-regard."

Self-esteem is not something that has to be learned. We all seem to have it in abundance in very early childhood. Later, as social forces act upon us, we soon learn that we do not always measure up to the various social or developmental standards imposed on us. In other words, the most primary conflict, producing anxious concern for all of us, begins early in life when we find out that the social judgments made of us are not always flattering or in keeping with our own more exalted sense of self-worth. Thus, gradually, self-regard (or self-loathing as it may become) develops as a matter of self-evaluation based on family and cultural values. For all of us, then, self-regard becomes socially mediated; we become, as Harry Stack Sullivan puts it, "the reflected appraisals of significant others."

As William McCall says so well, "It is reasonable to presume then, given the painful conflict that can be created between our innate sense of self-esteem and the more critical social appraisals made of us by others, that we should have some way of resolving the doubt, the contradiction thus generated about our self-worth."[3]

There seem to be two basic ways of safeguarding our self-esteem. Each has enormous consequences for the self-concept and the future adjustment of the person to reality. The first of these adjustive attitudes is called coping, the second is called defensiveness.

Coping implies that we realistically work out the discrepancy over self-worth, that we confront the conflict and modify our behavior to be more in accord with family and cultural expectations. Coping does not base self-esteem upon the childlike idealistic image of the perfect self, but values the self despite its imperfections and seeks to bolster self-esteem through realistic accomplishment.

The second way of dealing with a threat to self-worth is the path of defensiveness. It is a far easier path than coping because it evades the threat and nullifies it to some degree rather than facing up to the conflict and endeavoring to overcome it directly. The path of defensiveness leads to a kind of "automatic and indeliberate psychic manipulation" which sets defense above adjustment, and refusing to acknowledge the threat to self-esteem as a real threat, admits it like a Trojan horse into the citadel of the self. It is as though the adverse judgment of significant others or the detection of unacceptable qualities or dispositions in ourselves is so disruptive of self-esteem that it cannot be borne. We say to ourselves in effect, "Oh, no; that can't be true," and proceed to act as though it were not. At the same time, of course, there is some recognition that this unacceptable element might be true, otherwise it would constitute no threat.

In substance, then, the contradiction is at once denied and accepted, an impossible position to hold openly, as Freud brilliantly and profoundly saw. The human person, said Freud, can live with this contradiction only by suppressing one of its terms (rendering it "unconscious"), by deceiving himself into thinking that what is glimpsed as true is not true. It is perhaps Freud's greatest contribution to abnormal psychology to have penetrated so deeply into the workings and implications of this defensively determined initial self-deception. From this he went on to identify what he and his daughter, Anna, called the "ego-defense mechanisms," the various unconscious maneuvers by which the inner self seeks to defend its integrity against the imputation of unacceptable qualities and tendencies, and to show the importance of these maneuvers in the development of abnormal or peculiar habits or attitudes.

The Defense Mechanisms: Anna Freud is credited with first systematically describing the major defense mechanisms.4 They are faithfully described in outline form by Drellich in contemporary language.5 The following outline of the major defense mechanisms as described by both Drellich and McCall illustrates the placement of denial in the original nomenclature and shows that in the present language of alcoholism denial can also be equated with the very fundamental act of repression itself.

In the most fundamental sense, defense mechanisms are self-protective psychological maneuvers, largely unconscious, designed to soften or disguise what is unacceptable to the inner self. The basic goal is to protect the self against threats, real or imagined, from internal or external sources. While orthodox Freudians believe that the defense mechanisms are used primarily to protect the self against anxiety produced by unconscious aberrant sexual impulses, other behavior pathologists would maintain that whatever is threatening to our self-esteem is a fitting subject for cognitive/emotional self-defense. Further, it should be noted that to say the defense mechanisms are largely unconscious is to stress by implication that they are always in corresponding degree self-deceptive. As a matter of fact, if the individual were not taken in by them, McCall says, they would not serve to defend his or her self-esteem against the intimation of inadequacy or dereliction.

Repression is the most fundamental of defense mechanisms since, unless the self-devaluating memory or motive is somehow removed from the center of consciousness, it is difficult to see how we can be deceived into using other means to defend against it. All other mechanisms would thus seem to depend upon at least an initial repression. Basically, repression is the exclusion of an idea and its associated feelings from consciousness. It may exclude a thought that was once conscious but was too painful and had to be banished from conscious awareness. It may keep ideas or inclinations from ever reaching conscious awareness. Since there is much in our psychic life that is neither clearly conscious nor entirely unconscious, it is well to keep in mind that in discussing repression and the unconscious we are talking, at least at times, about repression that is only partially successful as well as unconscious mechanisms that can be made conscious with but modest effort. Basically then, repression is an attempt at exclusion from awareness of self-devaluating experiences such as shameful memories and unacceptable motives whether they are hostile, fearful, sexual, pettily selfish, crude, dishonest, or contemptible.

Isolation is the defense whereby ideas are split off from the feelings that are associated with and appropriate to them. The mechanism may be looked upon as an attempt to cut off or blunt the unacceptable aspects of a total experience. For example, a repeated thought, such as "my boss is going to have a serious accident," may be consciously experienced if that thought is isolated from its associated feelings of wishfulness and guilt about such an accident happening in the first place. Thus, the thought without the feeling component is experienced as an alien, intrusive idea that has no real connection with the person experiencing the thought. The defense of self-esteem by isolation is obvious; one can think the hostile thought without feeling the guilt that would accompany it if the appropriate hostile emotions were to be experienced.

Reaction formation is a largely unconscious attempt to replace an unacceptable drive or emotion with its almost polar opposite. Thus, in Freudian language, a person may remain entirely unaware of anal erotic impulses to make a great mess by maintaining a conscious, active concern with order, neatness, and cleanliness. Again, the goal is to defend one's self-esteem against unacceptable dispositions in the self.

Displacement refers to the unconscious tendency to direct an unacceptable wish away from the original object and onto an essentially neutral or less threatening object. Examples are numerous, as in the urge to kick the dog when we are angry at someone else.

Projection is the defense whereby a painful, unacceptable impulse or idea is attributed to someone else. To project is to defend self-esteem against unacceptable motives by attributing to others either the motives themselves or the criticism of oneself for having such motives. Thus, a young woman who cannot allow herself to recognize sexual feelings toward her married employer will be convinced that he is sexually interested in her and that he is communicating his interest in many indirect ways (primary projection). Or, in a more negative sense, she may view her employer as being very critical of her as a shallow, emotionally excitable young lady with an unacceptable value system (secondary projection). Obviously, what is projected in secondary projection is one's own self-devaluating attitudes.

Undoing represents an unconscious symbolic restitution or reparation whereby the individual makes unconscious amends for having thought or acted in an unacceptable, guilt-producing way. A distinction must be made between restitution as a conscious and deliberate social act designed to make up for a wrong, and the defense of undoing which can be a self-deluding "magical" act whereby we attempt to symbolically annul our delinquency. For example, an unscrupulous businessman may make generous charitable contributions to his church and thereby permit himself to continue his dishonest business practices at other times. Symbolically, with each charitable gift, he seemingly wipes the slate clean or pays the price of his dishonest practices only to start over again.

Denial is a very primitive defense in the nomenclature of Ego Psychology whereby the individual remains unaware of certain tangible, visible aspects of external reality that would be painful if acknowledged. It is best exemplified in many of us with the persistent feeling that the death of a loved one has not occurred and the deceased is still alive despite the obvious evidence to the contrary.

Rationalization is said to occur when a person is convinced that he or she is carrying out or avoiding an action for some neutral or acceptable reason in order to remain unaware of the unacceptable but largely unconscious motive that may lie behind the action. Expressed another way, rationalization may be described as a pseudo-explanation of a behavior or an attitude that substitutes an acceptable motive for an actual, more unacceptable one. Thus, the rationalizer may view idleness as needed relaxation, or cowardice as caution, or a severe need to discipline as being in the child's best interest.

Identification is difficult to describe because it is far more than a defense mechanism. Rather, it seems to be an almost total aspect of maturation and learning through which a child learns to become like another person, usually a loved or feared parent or parent substitute. By identification, the child acquires some of the values, mannerisms, behavioral styles, and sometimes even the pathological symptoms of the person identified with. In a narrower sense, the pathology of identification occurs when one unconsciously defends self-esteem against the conviction of inadequacy and weakness by viewing oneself as somehow the same as or one with some figure of power or status. Defensive identification reflects what the individual is not but would like to become as a means of escape from the self-devaluating reality of personal limitations.

Compensation: It was Alfred Adler who invented the term compensation. He saw clearly that every style of life demands the stressing of certain values and the subordination of others. He saw compensation as a normal socializing process. However, as an unconscious defense mechanism, compensation may be described as a defensive maneuver that enables us to offset unacceptable tendencies or weaknesses by overvaluing and overstressing acceptable motives or strengths. Since compensation is a relatively normal coping device, we only have the right to think of it as an unrealistic and unsightful or unconscious defense mechanism if devaluation of one goal or behavior is exaggerated as a means of defending self-esteem against some unconscious or unacknowledged imperfection.

Defensive devaluation: Although not listed in the Freudian nomenclature, this defense mechanism is so ubiquitous that it should be listed here. It seems that if we cannot compensate for weaknesses and transgressions, we can divert attention from them by concentrating on the faults of others. Though not included in the classical lists of defense mechanisms, defensive devaluation appears to be an important self-protective maneuver that involves focusing upon the weaknesses and aberrations of others as a means of calling attention away from our own deficiencies. Behaviorally, defensive devaluation involves unwarranted or unnecessary griping or gossiping about any number of people or things. As McCall says, "The defensive devaluator does not criticize in the hope of effecting reform, but as a defense against his or her own sense of inadequacy and perhaps guilt. The presence of repression is indicated by the individual's general insensitivity to faults in himself in the face of an extreme sensitivity to the inconsiderateness, stupidity, and similar faults of others. One sees only the mote in his neighbor's eye but misses the splinter in his own, and with a vengeance."[3]

It must be stressed that one's utilization of defense mechanisms is not to be automatically or arbitrarily equated with

Appendix 1

pathology. All humans beings need and use a variety of defense mechanisms, apparently without signs of serious mental or emotional disturbance. What is significant is the specific manner or style in which we use certain defense mechanisms and whether their utilization is within appropriate cultural norms.

The Psychology of Denial in Alcoholism

The Meaning of Denial in the Alcoholic: The term "denial" has a connotation in the field of alcoholism that goes far beyond the original definition of the term in the lexicon of ego psychology. Presently, denial is a shorthand term for a wide repertoire of psychological defenses and maneuvers that alcoholic persons unwittingly set up to protect themselves from the realization that they do in fact have a drinking problem. These defensive maneuvers, all of which distort reality, can appear in many different forms. Some of the most common are:[7]

Simple denial: Maintaining that something is not so which is in fact so, e.g., insisting that alcohol is not a problem despite obvious evidence that it is a problem and is so perceived by others. The alcoholic person's dishonesty is also a form of denial. He or she frequently does not tell the truth but is unaware of this.

Minimizing: Admitting, to some degree, a problem with alcohol or other drugs, but in such a way that it appears to be a much less serious or significant problem than is actually the case.

Blaming (also called projection): Denying responsibility for certain behavior and maintaining that the responsibility lies with someone or something else. The behavior is not denied, but its cause is placed "out there," not within the person.

Rationalizing: Offering alibis, excuses, justifications, and other explanations for behavior. These serve essentially to provide a reason other than alcoholism to explain behavior related to uncontrolled drinking or drug use. The behavior is not denied, but an inaccurate explanation of its cause is given.

Intellectualizing: Avoiding emotional, personal awareness of the problem of alcoholism by dealing with it on a level of generalization, intellectual analysis, or theorizing.

Diversion: Changing the subject to avoid a topic that is threatening, e.g., personal alcohol or drug usage and related behavior.

Hostility: Becoming angry and irritable when reference is made to personal chemical usage and related behavior. This is a good way to avoid the issue as it serves to back people off. If you are angry with them when they talk about a certain topic, people will change the subject or avoid bringing it up again.

Denial is automatic: Denial, in its various forms, is not usually a matter of deliberate lying or willful deception. It is a serious psychological mechanism that operates unconsciously. In most instances, alcoholic persons do not know what is true or false concerning their use of alcohol and its consequences. They are blinded to the fact that their view of the situation does not conform to reality. The denial system distorts their perception and impairs their judgment so that they become self-deluded, incapable of accurate self-awareness.

Denial is progressive: The denial system becomes more pervasive and entrenched as the illness of alcoholism continues to progress. In the very early stages, it is usually minimal and, with encouragement, such persons can usually view their problem

Appendix 1

fairly realistically with few distortions. However, by the time an individual's illness is sufficiently advanced that the problem appears serious to others, an elaborate system of defenses has usually been built up, blinding the alcoholic person to what is really happening. When a person passes from the middle to the late stage of alcoholism, the denial system is usually massive and extremely difficult to penetrate. The terminal stage alcoholic, for example, may be dying from cirrhosis of the liver yet denying any history of uncontrolled or excessive drinking.

The Meaning of Denial in the Family and Community

It has only been within the past decade that we have learned the shocking fact that the family of the alcoholic, as well as most concerned others, reacts to the alcoholism of a family member or friend in the same stereotyped fashion as a typical alcoholic. Again, it is the complex system of denial that is the major defensive maneuver.

How is this possible? Why do most concerned others, who do not have the condition, behave in the same way as the alcoholic and share some of the identical feelings and attitudes? Once again, self-esteem is socially mediated. Both the alcoholic and family live in a common culture, a culture that is extremely ambivalent about alcoholism. Perhaps our greatest barrier to understanding alcoholism is our culturally learned ambivalence and our need to avoid facing the issue of alcoholism. It is part of our cultural heritage. Whether we like it or not, all of us are faced internationally with the conflict produced by the classic temperance movement in the United States.[2] The outcome of this terrible wet-dry controversy is that most of us have avoided the conflict, denied it, not seen it, not talked about it, and hoped it would go away. This position has been called the conspiracy of silence, the deadly silence. It could just as well be called the deadly denial system.[7,8]

Here is how it works. The family, the peers, the friends, and the supervisors of the practicing alcoholic frequently fail to recognize the obvious signs and symptoms of the illness. We deny the illness concept and we tolerate chronic alcoholic behavior. We don't like the behavior we see in the alcoholic and we reject the alcoholic for this behavior, yet we silently tolerate it. This is called the rejection-enabling system. That is, we reject the alcoholic for his or her obstreperous behavior and yet that very act of rejection permits the alcoholic to continue behaving in this pathological fashion indefinitely. Thus, alcoholism typically develops and flourishes for 7–14 years on the average, well into the chronic phase, before it is recognized.

The shocking revelation here is that chronic alcoholism could not exist and be perpetuated without this kind of cultural support. It is now well known that almost every alcoholic has a partner. The partner may be a spouse, a peer, a friend, a relative, a colleague, or a supervisor, but a partner, nevertheless, that aids and abets the progression of the illness through the conspiracy of silence.[9,10]

By way of example, in our culture, family, friends, and peers make it easier for the alcoholic to drink to intoxication by denying that the drinking or behavior is abnormal, by covering up for mistakes and time off from work, by covering up the truth about the uncontrolled drinking, or by tolerating other obvious signs of alcoholism. The significant other may even fire or discharge the alcoholic employee or divorce the alcoholic spouse, but all of this is still part of the rejection-enabling system. Typically, family, friends, and peers do not get outside help for themselves to learn how to handle the situation, even though it has been perpetuated for years. They do not express directly to the alcoholic their concern about the evidence of intoxication or the harmful consequences of drinking which they have observed. Typically, they do not even mention that the local resources are available for help. Again, the deadly silence is at work: the failure to offer the alcoholic person an opportunity to learn about the effects of his or her behavior on other people.[7]

As a result of our growing awareness of the extensiveness of the denial system in the significant other, we have come to look upon families, friends, peers, and employers as persons who are very much like practicing alcoholics. For example, just as alcoholics deny that they have a drinking problem, the family and friends of alcoholics also refuse to accept it—despite its obvious visibility. Just as the alcoholic rationalizes and makes excuses for drinking, the family and friends of alcoholics often make excuses to themselves and to friends for the abnormal drinking instead of accepting the fact that the person is ill and needs treatment. Just as the alcoholic blames his or her drinking on other people and other problems, many families and friends are diverted by the alcoholic's excuses for drinking into believing that people and problems are to blame for the alcoholism. Thus, paradoxically, what we find in families is the same pathological reaction to alcoholism that we find in the practicing alcoholic. It would seem that this pathological denial process is as stable and consistent and predictable in the significant other as it is in the practicing alcoholic.

Overcoming Denial in Treatment Programs

Dealing with Denial in the Patient: In a very real sense it is denial that is the major barrier to recovery in alcoholism.[11] Because of its pervasive operation, most people enter treatment for alcoholism because of external pressures, not because they recognize they have a problem. Usually, some crisis in the family or at work brings the patient to treatment.

The extent of denial varies considerably among individuals. Some are totally blind to the existence of their illness. Others admit having the illness to some degree, but they virtually always fail to fully appreciate the extent, the seriousness, and/or the personal nature of the problem. Unless something happens to weaken the various defenses that comprise the denial system, they will not be willing or able to accept help in the difficult task of recovery.

Direct intervention: Experience in alcoholism rehabilitation shows that a direct approach to denial is most effective. That is, therapy should deal directly with the presenting problem, the alcoholic behavior that is resulting in harmful consequences. It should seek to deliberately and systematically interfere with the progression of the disease.

A direct approach does not deal with causation, since this strategy has been found to be nonproductive and actually to interfere with the initiation of recovery. Neither does it deal, at least initially, with other problems in the alcoholic individual's life. This direct approach is used for two basic reasons: (1) most other problems of the alcoholic individual usually stem directly or indirectly from the alcoholism, and (2) until the alcoholic person deals with this primary problem, he or she is not in a position to benefit from efforts to resolve problems in other areas. This is largely because the denial system makes alcoholics incapable of realistic awareness or meaningful effort regarding any of their life problems.

Since uncontrolled drinking is the immediate and obvious problem in cases of alcoholism, the rationale of a direct approach dictates that it must be the first focus of any rehabilitation effort. Initially, there is no concern with any other problems that may later become part of the ongoing treatment process. (There are some rare exceptions to this rule in cases where a severe concomitant medical or psychiatric disorder must be dealt with immediately before the treatment of the alcoholism can be attempted.) The primary goal of direct treatment, then, throughout the rehabilitation process, is to help affected persons utilize available techniques to stop the drinking or other drug use that is interfering with their functioning. However, such direct methods cannot be applied unless the patient is in a receptive frame of mind—a frame of mind that is not attainable as long as the denial system is operating.

The first stage in treatment: Following detoxification, the basic and ongoing priority in any continuing rehabilitation effort is the establishment of a caring attitude so that the alcoholic person feels accepted as a worthwhile individual. This is the necessary foundation upon which all effective efforts must stand. However, the prerequisite step in actual treatment is to begin coming to grips with denial. This is the most crucial step in rehabilitation for, unless denial is overcome, the alcoholic person will not become actively involved in recovery. It was not until Alcoholics Anonymous emphasized this point that its significance as a basic key to treatment was understood. It is still not widely known in most segments of our society, either lay or professional.

Obviously, people who are dependent on alcohol cannot begin to deal with this primary problem unless they first face up to the fact that they have the illness. Thus, the first task in rehabilitation is to bring the patient to the realization that alcoholism or some other form of addiction is the dominant reality of their lives. Only then can the person also be helped to learn to cope with this primary process in a constructive manner. Only then can the person be helped to deal with other life areas, such as psychological problems, family problems, and job problems, which will have some relationship with how well the person is able to learn to live with the illness.

As long as the denial system is intact, the alcoholic person is not concerned with doing anything appropriate about the problem. Thus, if the person is to become motivated, a high level of personal concern must be created; this can only be achieved by penetrating the denial system.

Strategies for Penetrating the Denial System: Modern alcoholism treatment programs are able to achieve a high degree of success in breaking down or reducing the denial system by an approach that combines two essential features: (1) surrounding alcoholic patients with care, concern, and understanding, and (2) providing them with a multitude of objective facts about their illness and its grim consequences.

Presentation of facts: Although alcoholic persons are usually unable to face their illness alone, they can face it with proper assistance. In part, such assistance consists of providing them with an education about the nature of their illness. Even more important, it consists of presenting them with the evidence of their personal excessive and/or inappropriate alcohol usage and the harmful consequences that resulted from it. Others who are knowledgeable about the illness and not blinded by their own denial system can help them see the objective realities of their situation in this way. Even other alcoholic patients who have only partially shed their own denial systems are in a good position to help with this, due to the seeming fact of human nature that we can always see another's problems more clearly than our own. Virtually all successful alcoholism rehabilitation programs, whether residential or community-based (such as A.A.[12]) provide such means of helping alcoholic persons face up to the facts of their illness.

Rehabilitation atmosphere: Presentation of facts is unlikely to penetrate the denial system unless psychological support is also provided. It seems to be of paramount importance that caregivers communicate that their primary motivation is care and concern for the patient. Since the moral stigma that our society has attached to alcoholism is one of the most significant factors in creating and sustaining the denial system, an entirely different attitude must be conveyed if there is to be success in dissolving or reducing it. Thus, there must be an absence of any aura of moralizing, accusation, condemnation, or punitiveness, as well as sympathy or pity. All of these attitudes reflect lack of understanding of the alcoholic person suffering from an illness. These attitudes work against positive change by almost guaranteeing that anyone receiving them will be unwilling to undergo the pain of facing their behavior.

Usually, alcoholic persons have never had a proper opportunity to experience this pain and then work through it in a constructive manner. Either the use of alcohol has short-circuited the hurting process or there has not been a caring, empathic, psychologically supportive environment to help see it through. Usually both of these factors operate to stand in the way of recovery; an effective rehabilitation program optimizes prospects for recovery by eliminating them. Whether residential or community-based, such a program is characterized by an approach that projects objectivity and empathy in dealing with the alcoholic person's denial system. Those who are trying to accomplish this convey the message that they have the person's best interest at heart, even if this means presenting facts that are painful to hear. In a context where the relationship to the alcoholic person is based on real understanding and acceptance, there is little chance that even a vigorous attack on the denial system will be perceived as moralistic or rejecting.

The stage sequential process of dealing with denial: Dealing with denial in a formal alcoholism treatment program is a systematic process that has certain basic characteristics whatever the setting or specific approach. The method, whether formal or informal, appears to involve three distinct (but in actual practice, overlapping) steps or stages:

1. Verification of the nature of the problem—this involves gathering information to verify that the individual is alcoholic. It requires collection of supporting evidence of a history of harmful consequences resulting from the use of alcohol or other mood-altering substances. It requires ruling out that this pattern of self-defeating behavior could reasonably be accounted for by any problem other than alcoholism.
2. Convincing the individual that the problem exists—that he or she is alcoholic. This goes beyond simple statements or labeling; it needs to incorporate objective evidence upon which the determination of the extent of the problem is based.
3. Convincing the person to do something about the problem—given agreement upon the nature of the problem, the person now needs help in making a decision to take action designed to remedy the problem.

The first two steps constitute the initial phase of treatment. The third phase begins later and continues throughout the remainder of the rehabilitation process, at first only at a superficial level and then in ever-increasing depth. The extent of time and energy required to penetrate and dissolve the denial system varies greatly from individual to individual. The material that follows indicates how the task would typically be approached in a modern alcoholism rehabilitation center.

Appendix 1

The Assessment Process: Verification of the Nature of the Problem

Almost all individuals who are referred for treatment of alcoholism do, in fact, show evidence of being alcoholic to some degree. Most show an overabundance of such evidence, indicating that for the greatest chance of a successful recovery much earlier intervention would have been desirable. However, since occasional inappropriate referrals do occur, it is important to verify that alcoholism is the problem interfacing with the individual's functioning. In addition, a careful assessment is necessary in order to establish the extent and severity of the illness and to develop a treatment plan suitable for the individual needs of each person.

Assessment of alcoholism is most successfully accomplished, and valid results are most often attained, when one's approach has the following characteristics: (1) it communicates nonjudgmental acceptance and objectivity, (2) it is patient and persistent, (3) it focuses on specifics, (4) it does not accept defensive maneuvers (e.g., alibis or rationalizations), (5) it aims to establish whether or not there is a significant connection between the person's drinking or chemical usage and repeated harmful consequences in various areas of his or her life, (6) it gives the individual feedback about the results of the assessment process citing the evidence for any conclusion of alcoholism that may be made.

Assessment Modalities: There are a variety of means by which assessment of alcoholism can be accomplished. All of the following are useful sources of data. The most valid determinations are those based on several kinds of information that serve to corroborate each other.

Formal interview: A comprehensive approach to assessment utilizes a systematic, focused, formal interview with the alcoholic patient. While more accurate information can usually be obtained from others, it is important to interview the individual patient if the goal is treatment of the illness. The purpose of the interview, which should be conveyed to the person being interviewed, is to review his or her life history in relation to use of alcohol as well as other mood-altering chemicals, and to establish whether or not there is a pattern of harmful alcohol or chemical usage.

Such an interview explores, in a structured and patterned manner, the individual's past and current alcohol or chemical use as it relates to harmful consequences in all areas of life: family life, social life, occupational functioning, legal problems as well as physical and mental health. The focus should be on adverse consequences resulting exclusively or primarily from the chemical usage. For example, it becomes important to determine whether a man abuses his wife only when he is drinking or whether he also does it when sober. In addition, the interview may assess the stage of alcoholism an individual has reached by means of specific questions relating to such issues as the Jellinek chart.[13] While this type of interview usually explores the amount, frequency, and type of the person's alcohol usage, this is not of primary concern. What is of major concern is the repetitive pattern of such usage, despite repeated harmful consequences.

It is usually very difficult to get meaningful information in these areas from alcoholic persons for at least three reasons: (1) the person usually has not shared this kind of material before; selected bits and pieces may have been revealed to others from time to time, but usually not to one person or all in one comprehensive package, (2) the person lacks insight into the material due to the profound effects of the denial system, (3) also because of the denial system, the person is long accustomed to being defensive and can rationalize and minimize the material very easily.

Interviewing techniques: The interviewer can best obtain reasonably accurate and relevant information by using the following techniques:

1. Use a businesslike, matter-of-fact approach.
2. Ask highly specific, factual questions that are difficult to answer with evasions or vague generalities.
3. Tactfully, but firmly and insistently, probe for factual details, never taking responses at face value or accepting vague and general answers.
4. Stick to the main task, focusing exclusively on the areas that need to be covered by the interview. Sidestepping or diversionary tactics, e.g., changing the subject, should not be permitted.
5. Never focus on the alibis, excuses, rationalizations, or other defensive or inaccurate explanations. Do keep helping the person to see the alcoholic behavior more clearly and factually.

This kind of interviewing is difficult and usually has to be learned. It requires an interviewer who is knowledgeable about the patterning of the illness of alcoholism, and some skill is required in utilizing the highly structured, directive approach that is necessary to cut through the denial system and get at relevant essentials. Most professionals are trained to use indirect interview methods that too easily allow alcoholic people to manipulate or avoid the issue. As a result, the interviewer is conned or backed off and fails to get accurate diagnostic information.

A direct interview benefits not only the interviewer who obtains the needed information, but also benefits the interviewee. Patients are provided with an opportunity to see for themselves the pattern that is emerging from their lives, and frequently its cumulative impact brings the dawning of a new insight into the existence of harmful alcohol or other chemical dependency of which they had been quite unaware. Feedback about the extensiveness and seriousness of this pattern, e.g., how far the illness has progressed, can also help patients to gain additional awareness.

Other data that can be obtained from individual patients might include additional signs and symptoms of alcoholism or drug dependency. Other systematic interviews attempt to assess additional related problems in the person's life that would merit consideration in developing an individualized treatment plan.

Observations of peer group: Strangely, one of the most effective ways of helping any given patient to break through the denial system is to put him or her in a close relationship with other people suffering from the same condition. Somehow, in both formal and informal meetings, fellow sufferers are able to help each other. This clearly happens in A.A. and is usually based on the "story" a new member tells, with other members making their own assessment of the problem based on this introductory message. The same thing happens in formal rehabilitation programs. A new person arrives on a treatment unit and those already there begin asking questions about why the new patient came to treatment and requesting other details of his or her story. Typically, the majority of patients in treatment have made varying degrees of progress in working through their own denial system and are aware, at least to some degree, of their own alcoholism and of the high probability that any new arrival has the same problem. Most are by now quite knowledgeable about the illness, both from their own personal experiences and from the education they have been receiving during treatment, so they know it is helpful to "zero in" on the new person's alcohol or chemical history. Peers are usually very good at asking appropriate questions and, because they also have the problem, are generally very sensitive to the importance of being accepting and nonmoralistic. For the same reason, they are not likely to be fooled by defensive maneuvers.

Information from other sources: Because of their denial system, information received from alcoholic persons themselves is usually not very reliable. To get a more valid assessment of the extent and seriousness of the illness, corroborating information should be obtained from others who have been closely involved with that individual. This can be done by interviews and questionnaires, all with the patient's permission, of course.

This requires contacting the person's family and/or significant others whose close relationship to that person puts them in the best position to give a detailed history. The information from significant others is also subject to considerable distortion because of their own denial system and emotional involvement in the matter. However, their view is almost certain to be more accurate than that of the alcoholic patient, simply because the latest crisis became so significant that they were required to insist on the patient formally going for treatment. Also, since alcoholism so deeply affects family members, communicating with them means including these key surrounding persons in the rehabilitation process from the very beginning. Since chances of recovery are greatly increased when they are involved, it is best if this happens as soon as possible.

Other valuable information may also be obtained from the patient's employer, physician, and any individual or agency involved in previous efforts to intervene in the alcoholism. Of course, this information would only be obtained with the patient's permission.

Convincing the Person That the Problem Exists

Once the data have been gathered, and the nature and extent of the alcoholic problem established, the next goal is to help people comprehend one central reality—the fact of their illness. They must become convinced that they have this problem. The more complete the denial, the greater will be the struggle to break through it. For the alcoholic person, "accepting reality is tantamount to working to maintain sobriety and it is simply unreasonable to expect someone with a profound dependence on a chemical substance to give it up without a struggle."[14]

Confrontation: Denial is overcome by presentation of facts—confrontation. This is accomplished in part by education about the nature of the illness. But more than that, alcoholic people must become convinced that this illness is a personal reality. They usually admit drinking or even using other drugs and admit that they have problems, but do not admit that these two things go together. They also tend to deny or underestimate the adverse effects of chemical usage on their lives. Experience indicates that others can systematically help them work through these self-deceptions by reviewing their own life experiences with them and by confronting them with the objective realities of their situation.

Characteristics of effective confrontation: While not exhaustive, the following approach to confrontation, developed through experience, seems to be of value:

1. It should be objective, firm, and nononsense, sticking with factual descriptions. It should avoid opinions or suppositions as well as any implications of moralizing or attacking.
2. It should be specific and personalized in such a way that it could only be referring to that person's life and no other.
3. It should have considerable depth and breadth, giving the person opportunities to examine and reexamine all available relevant evidence. It should cover a combination of harmful consequences and a wide range of life areas including physical, psychological, social, vocational, and spiritual damage to the person's life and explicitly correlate these problems with drinking or other drug usage.
4. It should emphatically point out the implications of this behavioral evidence. That is, the person should be presented with the inescapable conclusion, based on the accumulation of harmful consequences resulting from the alcoholism, that his or her behavior fits the description of an alcoholic person. Its message says, "You act like an alcoholic person because you are one." This conclusion, in turn, is strongly supported with the corroborating evidence.
5. It should be appropriately insistent and persistent to whatever extent is indicated by the strength of the person's defenses. Individuals attempting to confront must refuse to enable the

continuance of the denial system by refusing to accept the various defenses that will virtually always be encountered in one form or another, such as denial, minimizing, rationalizing, blaming, or excusing. They must be firm and steadfast in maintaining that there are no valid reasons for an alcoholic person to drink or to continue to use other mood-altering substances.

6. It should emphasize that, while the person may have other problems in his or her life, as long as the alcoholism goes untreated, these other problems cannot be solved but only aggravated and perpetuated.

"Tough love": Although it may appear that a confrontive approach is incompatible with the caring attitude that has been described as essential to successful treatment of alcoholism, the two can be very productively combined. Confrontation is judgmental in a sense but it is a nonmoralistic, nonrejecting approach that has the key elements of empathic understanding and acceptance. Appropriate confrontation is an attack in a sense, but not on the person; the attack is on his or her facade of defenses. When care and concern for the person are present, and when there is a foundation of communication and rapport, it is possible to be quite forceful in encouraging patients to abandon their resistances and come to a more realistic and honest appraisal of themselves and their condition.[14]

Actually, it is care and concern that motivate other concerned people to insist that alcoholics face themselves. Experience in treating alcoholic persons indicates that only by coming to know the truth about their illness can they begin to move in a more constructive direction. To fail to help them do this is a disservice, allowing the continuation of a disorder that is ultimately fatal. To help them do this, even if it is a painful process, is caring for them as human beings deserve to be cared for. Such an approach is often called "tough love."

Goal of in-depth awareness: To be effective, confrontation must go beyond the superficial level, beyond a simple admission of the problem or a simple agreement with the assessment. The principal goal is to bring the person to the realization that he or she is caught up in an unpredictable, uncontrolled pattern of behavior. Only this realization can arouse enough concern to bring about adequate motivation for a serious attempt at recovery.

All alcoholic persons must eventually be helped to reach an in-depth awareness of their illness and its seriousness, a realization that has been described as a double disillusionment about the role of alcohol in their lives. This means not only disillusionment regarding the consequences of personal chemical usage but also about chemicals as a way of coping with the pain resulting from these consequences. It especially means coming to a realization of the following:

1. That the illness has been progressive, that life has increasingly centered around alcohol, and that the harmful effects have become more and more frequent and serious with the passage of time.
2. That its course will continue downhill to even more disastrous consequences unless something is done to arrest the progression.
3. That previous attempts at abstaining or controlling drinking or other chemical usage have been unsuccessful, demonstrating a powerlessness in this respect. (During the active stages of the illness, alcoholic individuals almost always focus on temporarily

successful attempts at control, ignoring the much more common loss of control. They must see that the chemical has been controlling them, not vice versa, and must come to the conviction that any compromise solution or controlled usage is not possible for them.)

The ultimate goal is that the cumulative impact of evidence drawn from their own history with alcohol will completely convince alcoholic persons that at all times and under all conditions, alcohol or other drugs produce more pain than pleasure for them. This conviction comes only gradually, in most cases, and is something that must be reinforced throughout the ongoing rehabilitation process.

Indications of success: Confrontation of the denial system is most likely to have a persuasive impact when it comes via a number of modalities. Most modern treatment programs employ structured conferences with rehabilitation staff members, peer group meetings, lectures, movies, and reading assignments, as well as conferences with concerned family members. Generally, these techniques help in penetrating the denial system.

There are several basic changes in an alcoholic person's behavior while in treatment that point to at least some degree of success in dissolving the denial system. These signs may occur after any of the modes of confrontation have taken place. Typical signs include the following:

1. The person is more able to acknowledge that his or her primary problem is alcoholism. There are fewer attempts to call the problem something else, such as a marital problem, a job problem, or just nervousness.
2. The person appears to be less defensive—there is less evidence of denying, minimizing, rationalizing, blaming, and so on.
3. The person seems able to volunteer new data about his or her alcohol or other chemical usage and resulting harmful consequences, data that are not in the possession of the treatment staff or peer group. Particularly impressive in this regard are data that could be known to no one but the alcoholic person, data that could have easily remained unknown and unshared.
4. The person seems more able to accept the immediate, present reality of the drinking problem and less concerned with the causes of it. Experience also shows that patients who keep insisting they must find out why they became alcoholics have not really recognized that they have the illness of alcoholism. Most of the time, seeking their underlying causes is a veiled attempt to find out the "cause" of their drinking so that they will be able to regain control and continue using the substance. Dwelling on causes, it seems, is a futile search in any case, and actually interferes with the recovery process.
5. The person is able to become willing to take some action to do something about his or her primary illness.

Appendix 1

Convincing the Person to Take Action

Awareness and understanding are of little use unless they are followed by action. The phase of initiating action begins as soon as the alcoholic person starts to face the reality of the illness. It merges into later phases of the rehabilitation process and is of an ongoing nature.

Even if the problem is initially acknowledged in only a tentative fashion, an effort must begin to convince the alcoholic to do something about the problem. Often, much persuasion and encouragement are required here, especially if the person is resistant or demoralized. The motivation to take action is most effectively mobilized when alcoholic persons are presented with a strong and united front by those around them. In modern treatment programs, whether residential or community-based, this generally comes through the combined efforts of staff and peer group, as well as through significant others in the alcoholic person's life.

Presenting alcoholic persons with their options is one of the most useful methods of bringing about constructive action at any stage of the recovery process. It is important that they be made aware that there is a choice either to continue on a course of progressive deterioration and self-destruction or to decide to do something systematic about the problem in order to avert this. When the denial system has been penetrated in an in-depth fashion, there is almost automatically a decision to take constructive action. For those who are not fully in touch with the extent, severity, and progressiveness of their illness, presenting the choice in this fashion can help tip the balance.

Deciding to take constructive action early in the rehabilitation process is not usually an in-depth choice. It is essentially a decision to become involved in recovery simply because there is no other viable alternative. While the problem is now being admitted, this does not necessarily imply an acceptance of the illness or of the means that will be required to make a recovery. In fact, it does not usually involve these, which develop later as the recovery process continues. The decision to take action at this stage is merely a decision to begin treatment in a meaningful sense, participating actively rather than passively or unwillingly. Sometimes this change is signaled when a person who has been wanting to leave the treatment setting makes the choice to remain.

Up to this point, the person's motivation almost always has been primarily external, stemming from outside pressures. At this point, internal motivation takes over and the individual actually becomes personally involved in his or her own rehabilitation. Only after this has happened do alcoholic persons become open to modifying their lifestyles in a manner conducive to living without alcohol or other mood-altering chemicals. It is only after this point that they become open to developing an awareness of their broader characteristics and problems as human beings, a development important to the next stages of rehabilitation.

Dealing with Denial in the Significant Other

Family Program: In recent years it has been increasingly recognized that the families of alcoholics can benefit by being involved in a treatment process specifically designed for them. "Family," as used here, refers to everyone who knows and cares about an alcoholic person. This may include family members, neighbors, employers, friends, supervisors, and others. For a rehabilitation program to be complete, some form of assistance for the family should be available, because these people are also part of the denial system and are suffering the pain that denial produces in them.[15,16]

The rationale for the treatment of family members is clear. While the alcoholic patient in treatment is learning a new way of life, a new way of coping with life without alcohol, there is usually no one around to help family members modify their denial system and other maladaptive attitudes and responses to the alcoholic's behavior. Thus, for both the alcoholic and the significant other, the problem to be faced is very similar: the problem is not the primary illness as much as it is the pathological response to the primary illness. One of the major goals of family intervention is to help the various significant others to stop making the same historic, culturally learned defensive responses as were being made by their alcoholic spouse, friend, or partner.[17, 18]

Family programs are geared to help family members identify their own attitudinal problems, to modify their defensive behavior where necessary, and to educate them about what to expect when the patient returns home. Family programs also teach significant others how to stop centering their lives around the alcoholic and instead detach from the alcoholism while still loving the person. Another objective of family programs is to help significant others to let the alcoholic's problems be his/hers and to start to live their own lives fully.

Family programs are generally short-term and may be inpatient or outpatient in structure. The program may consist of orientation sessions to acquaint the family members with the program followed by educational lectures and group therapy sessions whereby the participants can share experiences with others who are involved in similar family situations. Denial of the illness by the significant other has repeatedly been found to be the major barrier to recovery.

Appendix 1

Ongoing Nature of the Denial System

The most perplexing and pervasive aspect of the denial system is that, even after it has apparently been quite thoroughly eradicated, it can recur. This is part of the chronic nature of the illness of alcoholism. At any time, days or years later, there can be a resurgence of alibis, rationalizations, and other defense mechanisms that undermine realistic self-awareness. Unchecked, these defensive maneuvers sooner or later lead alcoholic persons back into the delusion that their illness does not exist, resulting in relapse.[19, 20] Thus, the task of dealing with denial in recovery means not only dissolving the denial system, but keeping it dissolved. It is an ongoing problem that requires lifelong vigilance and effort, with continual focus on attaining and maintaining self-honesty. This is one of the main reasons why alcoholic persons need an ongoing, long-term involvement in a health maintenance program which will ensure their lasting recovery. This, of course, is the program and fellowship of Alcoholics Anonymous.[12]

Endnotes

1. Anderson, D. J. *A History of Our Confused Attitudes Toward Beverage Alcohol,* Hazelden Foundation, Center City, Minnesota, 1968.
2. Lender, M. A., and K. R. Karnchanapee, "Temperance Tales," in *Journal of Studies on Alcohol,* Vol. 38, No. 7, 1977.
3. McCall, R. G. "The Defense Mechanisms Re-examined: A Logical and Phenomenal Analysis." *Cath. Psych. Records,* Vol. 1, No. 1, 1963, pp. 45–64.
4. Freud, A. *Ego and the Mechanisms of Defense,* International Universities Press, 1936.
5. Drellich, M. G. "Classical Psychoanalytic School" in S. Arieti (Ed.) *American Handbook of Psychiatry,* Second Ed., Basic Books, New York, 1974, pp. 751–52.
6. *The Caring Community Series, Dealing with Denial,* No. 6, Hazelden Foundation, Center City, Minnesota, 1975.
7. Weinberg, J. R. *The Deadly Silence, Friendship and Drinking Problems,* Hazelden Foundation, Center City, Minnesota, 1976.
8. Weinberg, J. R. *Why Do Alcoholics Deny Their Problem?* Hazelden Foundation, Center City, Minnesota. (Reprinted from *Minnesota Magazine,* August 1973.)
9. Kellermann, J. L. *Alcoholism, A Merry-go-round Named Denial,* Hazelden Foundation, Center City, Minnesota, Reprinted 1980.
10. Williams, T. *Crossing the Thin Line Between Social Drinking and Alcoholism,* Hazelden Foundation, Center City, Minnesota, 1979.
11. United States Department of Health, Education and Welfare and National Institute on Alcohol and Alcohol Abuse: *Third Special Report to the U.S. Congress on Alcohol and Health* from the Secretary of Health, Education and Welfare, June 1978, Technical Support Document, p. 274.
12. *Alcoholics Anonymous,* Alcoholics Anonymous World Services, Inc., New York, 1976.
13. Jellinek, E. M. "Phases of Alcohol Addiction," in *Quarterly Journal of Studies on Alcohol,* Vol. 13, No. 4, pp. 673–84, December 1952.
14. Keller, J. E. *Ministering to Alcoholics.* Minneapolis: Augsburg Publishing House, 1966.
15. Silver, R. *Reaching Out to the Alcoholic and the Family,* Hazelden Foundation, Center City, Minnesota, 1977.
16. *Al-Anon Faces Alcoholism,* Al-Anon Family Group Headquarters, Inc., New York, 1977.
17. Swift, H. A., and T. Williams. *Recovery for the Whole Family,* Hazelden Foundation, Center City, Minnesota, 1975.
18. Wright, K. D., and T. B. Scott. "The Relationship of Wives' Treatment to the Drinking Status of Alcoholics," in *Journal of Studies on Alcohol,* Vol. 39, No. 9, 1978.
19. Crewe, C. W. *A Look at Relapse,* Hazelden Foundation, Center City, Minnesota, 1974.
20. Solberg, R. J. *The Dry Drunk Revisited,* Hazelden Foundation, Center City, Minnesota, 1980.

BEHAVIORAL MANAGEMENT
OF CHRONIC ILLNESS
by

Daniel J. Anderson, Ph.D.

©1986, 1991 by Hazelden Foundation All rights reserved. Published 1986 Revised 1991.
(Originally titled *Living with a Chronic Illness*.)

Introduction

For some years, I have felt that the illness of alcoholism has been largely ignored, denied, rejected, and left untreated by society for two reasons: it represents not only unacceptable social behavior (drunken comportment), but also unacceptable pathological behavior (chronicity and incurability). In my view, it is the chronicity of alcoholism that we stigmatize, reject, and find contemptible, and not merely the condition of excessive or inappropriate alcohol use itself.

To explore this perspective, I became concerned with chronic illnesses other than alcoholism. How do people—both the sufferer and the family members—manage to live with other chronic illnesses? Do people with chronic illness respond to their condition with behavior similar to that of alcoholics? How do professionals handle chronic illness? Do we too ignore, deny, reject, or leave untreated not only alcoholics but people with other chronic illnesses as well? Are there any strategies or commonalities of coping or caring in the literature on chronic illness that might be effective in helping anyone living with this burden?

The following findings represent an ongoing attempt to explore this ambiguous and ubiquitous area of disability. It should be pointed out that there are a number of language problems that will frequently cause difficulty. Let me illustrate a few.

Many people who have a chronic illness do not want to be referred to as "victims," yet the professional literature frequently uses this term. For example, Mr. Smith could be referred to as a "victim" of rheumatoid arthritis, yet the heroic struggle he is making to continue to live a full life despite his disease defies use of the term victim. As an alternative, I have used the word *sufferer* in places, although it sounds somewhat stilted. Thus it might be better to say "a person who suffers from rheumatoid arthritis," or "a person or patient who has this disease."

The issue becomes even more complicated when one speaks of conditions, disorders, disabilities, or diseases. Broadly speaking, these terms are interchangeable. Yet at the same time, each has a more specific meaning in professional circles. For example, mental illnesses are properly identified as "disorders," while physical illnesses are called "diseases." But then, what is an "illness" or a "sickness"?

Obviously, there are different ways of being "sick." I like the straightforward way that Kleinman handles the problem, although there are other, more complex

Appendix 2

approaches.[1] The following is a summary of his thoughtful terminology:

- Disease: An illness that the medical/psychiatric professional recasts in terms of current theories about various disorders or disabilities; the professional interpretation of the health problem within a particular nomenclature and taxonomy; a particular disease nosology. Disease is a formally defined health problem—from the practitioner's point of view.
- Illness: Signs, symptoms, and suffering; generally, how the person, family, and friends live with the disability. Illness is a much more general problem from the point of view of the sick person and the significant other.
- Sickness: The broad understanding of a disorder in a comprehensive sense across a population and in relation to a variety of macrosocial forces, such as social perception, economic cost, and the like.[2]

Background

Health and longevity mean a great deal to us. According to Stokes, people living in developed nations have two major health concerns: how long they will live and how often they will be sick.[3] Paradoxically, people who live in modern industrial societies eat too much, smoke too much, drink too much alcohol, use too many other mood-altering substances inappropriately, work too hard without enough exercise, and live with too much stress. Thus despite our apparent concern about health and longevity, it seems we don't take good care of ourselves. In fact, a considerable body of literature suggests that many of our present-day illnesses are directly related to unhealthy lifestyles.[4]

At the same time, the major health care concern of most governments in developed countries is constantly rising health care costs and thus the urgent need for cost-containment measures. In the United States, health care expenditures are escalating very rapidly. National health care costs reached the $500-billion level in 1987, a 9.8 percent increase for the year. In relation to the economy, this figure represents an expenditure of 11.1 percent of the nation's total output of goods and services, called the gross national product (GNP). As recently as 1979, this proportion was only about 8.5 percent. The Commerce Department estimates that national spending on health care will be $756.3 billion in 1991, $80 billion more than in 1990. Pressure to quell this cost crisis is intensive. It comes from federal and state levels of government, from health care economists, from third-party insurance carriers, from business and industry health benefits managers, and from consumers. Nevertheless, assuming that the present incentive system of health care supply and demand remains substantially unchanged, total expenditures for health care in the United States are projected to reach 12.5 percent of the GNP over the next five years. Relatively speaking, the United States currently spends more than any other nation on health care. Rising health care costs are likely to remain a perplexing problem for or the foreseeable future.[5]

Recent cost-reduction responses from the health care and health insurance industries include the following:

- the development of ambulatory medical-surgical centers
- the creation of a variety of health maintenance organizations
- the creation of preferred-provider incentives
- the broadening of health services through multi-institutional systems and corporations
- the increased use of home health care services
- the development of government-monitored prospective payment systems
- the placing of limits on the use of diagnostic services
- the shifting of a larger share of costs to the consumer

However, even if implementing these strategies results in some degree of cost containment, wary investigators fear that the pressure to reduce health care costs may give rise to a number of new problems. The commercialization of health care may reduce needed personal services. Price competition may reduce the overall quality of care. Ethical problems related to economic priorities also arise. For instance, who does or does not have the right to which kinds of health care services? In other words, who will live and who will die?[6]

The ideal solution to rising health care costs is prevention. Finding more effective ways to prevent illness would include focusing more on major physical and mental health care problems and spending more on prevention than the estimated 4 percent of the health care dollar.[7] Despite the fact that many knowledgeable people are concerned about the need for more and better prevention studies and services, this critically needed and cost-saving approach to health care is still in its infancy. Why? Staying well is an essentially behavioral activity that is much more complex than it appears to be at first glance, and researchers are still debating the linkage between lifestyle and health.[8]

Since prevention is not the direct focus of this pamphlet, the complex issues involved will not be treated here. But the following analysis will take a closer look at one factor that affects all health care, whether one is dealing with primary prevention or secondary or tertiary intervention. This critical factor is the duration or degree of chronicity of illness and its usually devastating psychological and social impact on the patient, the friends and relatives, and the professional helpers.

The first step in this analysis involves differentiating acute illness from chronic and examining the typical positive and negative coping responses to chronic illness. The second step is a brief description and appraisal of an emerging network of self-care and mutual-help group activities that appear to be of increasing value to people coping with chronic illness. The third step is a very tentative discussion of some ideas for improving the effectiveness of this emerging collaborative network.

The differentiation between acute and chronic illness

Acute illness

Several sources agree on the most common characteristics of acute illness:

1. There is usually an abrupt onset.
2. The illness is limited in time, and the inconvenience is temporary.
3. Remission or death occurs in a short time.
4. Pain and suffering are limited, at least in duration.
5. Financial hardship is limited, at least in duration.
6. People with acute illnesses and their significant others maintain personal and social acceptability regardless of the outcome of the illness.
7. The focus is on the event, the immediate treatment, and cure of the disease, not on a long-term process of living with a chronic, disabling condition.[9]

In a historic sense, the best examples of acute illness are the infectious diseases such as tuberculosis, influenza, pneumonia, and diphtheria. Until about forty or fifty years ago, these were the great killers. But now, lifesaving drugs are available. Without question, modern medical and scientific technology must be credited with this advance.

Acute illnesses respond very well to the approach to treatment referred to as the basic "medical model." The significant sequential and interpersonal relationships of the medical model are as follows:

1. The illness is found to be disabling to a large number of people.
2. The causal agent is identified as an outside force, such as a germ, virus, or bacteria.
3. The sufferer is not held personally responsible for contracting the illness.
4. Professional technology and expertise dominate the caregiving.
5. A cure is usually effected with the use of a drug or therapy—and some people die.
6. With few exceptions, the patient-

as-victim is a relatively passive and naive beneficiary of care throughout the course of treatment.
7. The professional caregiver, on the other hand, remains relatively active, knowledgeable, and in control.[10]

The professional treatment of acute illness using the medical model and the accompanying fee-for-service reimbursement schedules are closely identified with the treatment of illness in general. Usually this is how modern professional health care is defined.

Chronic illness

Chronic illness seems to be a radically different phenomenon from acute illness, for everyone involved. The following are some common characteristics of chronic illness:

1. There is usually a more gradual onset than with acute illness.
2. The illness is of indefinite duration.
3. The illness may develop insidiously.
4. The condition may come and go episodically.
5. Remission or death may not occur for a very long time.
6. There may be great pain and suffering, at least periodically.
7. Financial hardship may be of astronomical proportions, even with health insurance.
8. Despite the fact that the condition is neither fatal nor curable, there may be intermittent or even constant threat of increasing disability or death.

Some of the best contemporary examples of chronic illnesses that are severe enough to impair include cancer, heart disease, hypertension, arthritis, diabetes, asthma, emphysema, kidney disease, chronic pain resulting from any cause, stroke, multiple sclerosis, the physical and mental debilitation associated with aging, the experience of death and dying, mental illness, and alcoholism and other drug addictions. And it appears that AIDS patients are living longer, even though the illness is presently incurable.

There are two main reasons why these chronic illnesses do not respond well to the acute illness model, to the medical model, to the fee-for-service reimbursement schedule, or to the be-cured-or-die model. On the one hand, physicians and other professionals are trained primarily to administer treatment and observe rapid results in the clinical course of an acute illness. On the other hand, patients are not well trained to cope with a chronic illness.[11]

One of the primary reasons that differentiating acute from chronic illness is so important is that chronic illness, as a percent of all illness, is rapidly emerging as a major health care burden. Lowell Levin of Yale University states that "it still seems the consensus of epidemiologists that the level of chronic disease in the 1930's and early 1940's was about 30 to 35 percent while today the picture remains one of about 80 to 85 percent chronic (not including mental illness)." Even allowing for some validity problems resulting from shifting definitions of diseases, the fact remains, he says, "that disease patterns have shifted significantly and that raises certain possibilities for self-care (and some policy issues as well)."[12] Expressed in terms of health care cost, the proportions are similar: "Eighty percent of health care resources in the United States, including facilities, services and biomedical research, are now devoted to chronic disease," says L. E. Cluff in a paper on chronic disease.[13]

The tragedy of chronic illness

Perhaps one of the greatest human needs is to be in full control of all our physical, mental, and emotional functions and thus be able to act freely in seeking out life-fulfilling, life-enhancing experiences. While all disabling illness interferes with or acts as a barrier to fulfilling such human needs, the potentially devastating psychological and social impact of chronic illness is particularly poignant for most people.

Investigators have suggested several factors that can seriously demoralize both the person with the chronic condition and family or friends:[14]

1. In chronic illness, the condition is often significantly and permanently disabling. The experience of living can be sharply and fundamentally restricted.
2. There is little hope of cure in chronic illness. This means that people who live with a chronic condition must somehow live with the fact that there is no real possibility of recovery, that the illness will not go away, and that it will probably linger indefinitely as a permanent disability. There is irrevocable loss.
3. In chronic illness, the specific condition largely determines one's lifestyle. The illness is in control. Depending upon the type of illness, one's behavior becomes increasingly stereotypical, repetitive, maladaptive, or compensatory. Choice and flexibility are sharply reduced.
4. The cause or causes of chronic illness are complex and often ambiguous. While vulnerability to both acute illness and chronic illness may involve multiple disposing factors (e.g., genetic, nutritional, psychological), the onset of an acute infectious illness is usually due to a germ or virus. Thus blame is on an outside agent. The major causes of chronic illness, however, are often related to a person's lifestyle, such as exercise level, salt intake,

tobacco and alcohol use, and so forth. Thus blame or attribution may be on the internal agent, the self. Consequently, the person may have strong guilt feelings because he or she violated rules of good health. Negative feelings may also result from judgments such as "I should have taken better care of myself."

5. The symptoms of chronic illness are frequently unpredictable and ambiguous. With some chronic diseases, there may be no observable symptoms. With cancer, rheumatoid arthritis, and alcoholism, the symptoms may disappear during periods of remission. With hypertension, heart disease, and alcoholism, there may be no observable symptoms until the disease has reached an advanced stage. And with many chronic illnesses, even though the person may believe he or she is cured when the illness is in remission, it is still present and active. Alcoholism and heart disease are perhaps the two best examples.

6. Again, because the symptoms in certain chronic illnesses are ambiguous, there may be long periods of struggle with false, improper, or changing diagnoses and treatment regimens.

7. Interpersonal relationships can become strained and difficult. All concerned may struggle with helping the sick person to find an appropriate balance between invalidism and independent functioning. A simple question like "How do you feel today?" may be difficult to answer. The sick person must decide how much to hide or how much to reveal, according to the situation.

8. Chronic illness produces not only self-blame, but shame as well. It stamps one as being somehow different or seriously limited as a human being. In chronic illness, shame is the experience of viewing the self as being unacceptably limited, deficient, or disvalued.

Loss of control

What might be the single most devastating psychological impact of chronic illness? What might be its most tragic characteristic? In a general sense, it is perhaps the repeated threat, or actual loss, of control over significant portions of one's life. For example, imagine the psychic pain one might experience after learning that a significant physical or mental function vital to one's sense of adequacy was threatened with impairment or was actually impaired, and that as a result, one's destiny was to live with increasing levels of relative helplessness and dependence upon others for daily needs. Thus one major consequence is the loss of a significant physical or mental function accompanied by the awareness that one is in a state of increased limitation and relative helplessness, and that one must submit to increased dependence on others for daily needs to survive.

Granting that almost all chronic disabling illnesses demand that people cope with various levels of human helplessness and limitation and various levels of impaired control over vital functions, it seems fair to conclude that the patient's personal response to this loss of control may significantly influence not only his or her quality of life, but perhaps even the outcome of the illness itself.

Thus inasmuch as how one responds to a chronic illness greatly affects one's quality of life, it is largely a personal behavioral problem.

Some pathological responses to chronic illness

How do people respond to the tragedy of chronic illness? To the pain and suffering? To the helplessness, the uncertainty, the ambiguity? To the unpredictability, the loss of control? How do they respond to the shame and guilt, the hopelessness? Considering the total negative impact of being faced with chronic illness—the physical burden, the psychological burden, the social burden, the spiritual burden—what frequently happens to people? A growing body of literature identifies a number of common pathological responses:[15]

1. Patients ignore obvious symptoms or adopt a wait-and-see attitude.
2. They diagnose and medicate themselves or consult a layperson.
3. They tend to delay or completely avoid seeking professional diagnosis and treatment.
4. They seek professional help only in medical or psychiatric emergencies.
5. When they do seek professional help, they want symptomatic treatment.
6. They deny that the illness is chronic.
7. They do not always follow expert advice.
8. They do not always follow medication instructions or prescribed medical routines.
9. They minimize or rationalize their reduced ability to cope or function as effectively as before.
10. They respond to the experience of chronic illness with shock, helplessness, depression, grief, demoralization, loss of self-esteem, guilt, shame, anger, resentment, self-pity, or self-loathing.
11. They may respond with behavioral extremes of childish dependency and helpless inadequacy, or defiant independence and arrogant grandiosity.
12. They become preoccupied with themselves and regress into a state of narcissistic entitlement; that is, they become finicky, demanding, and perfectionistic, expecting perfection from everything and everybody.

13. They become preoccupied with maintaining control over their internal psychological environment and their external social and physical environment. In fact, they try to manipulate and control everything. The tragedy is that as their loss of control increases, their need to maintain control also increases.
14. Not only does the chronic illness itself distress the patient, but his or her various pathological responses to the illness may produce even more stress.

How the sufferer responds to the illness may also have profound effects on how significant others respond—both to the person and to the illness—in terms of sympathy, empathy, caring, concern, avoidance, denial, hostility, and indifference.[16]

Some healthy coping responses to chronic illness

Despite growing evidence that many people react pathologically to chronic illness, there is also increasing evidence that other people (both the patient and significant others) are finding ways to modify such responses. Perhaps it has always been so, but until a few years ago, open discussion of chronic disease, death, and dying was repressed or at least strongly inhibited in our culture. Since the publication of Elisabeth Kübler-Ross's *On Death and Dying,* discussions of these topics have been much more open and uninhibited, and it is she who must be credited with first opening our eyes to the reality of incurable illness.[17]

Edwin J. Kenney, Jr., writing in *Commonweal,* traces the history of this growing willingness to face up to the ultimate tragedies in life by systematically reviewing the published accounts narrated by the sufferers themselves.[18] These authentic personal accounts of the tragedy of living with chronic illness or impending death include John Gunther's *Death Be Not Proud,* Betty Rollins's *First You Cry,* Cornelius and Kathryn M. Ryan's *A Private Battle,* Martha Weinman Lear's *Heartsounds,* Jeannie Morris's *Brian Piccolo: A Short Season,* and Norman Cousins's *Anatomy of an Illness.* All of these narrative descriptions try to make sense out of the experience of chronic illness and the suffering that accompanies it.

How does one find redemption in such tragic suffering? According to Kenney, most of the personal narratives take the following form:

> A "great" person in the common sense of one filled with life and talent and promise struggles heroically against disease, an enemy, a fate, which may ultimately vanquish the person. But in the disorder, suffering, and death of the tragic conflict, living itself and the values that give

life meaning are affirmed-love and work and the possibilities of community, of caring. Illness reveals to the people in these books not only what being alive in the world feels like, but also what it means to them. . . . Ultimately, these books are concerned with how to live, and how to bear the unbearable.[19]

How does one bear the unbearable? How does one continue to face up to extreme suffering, both physical and psychological? Kenney concludes his review of these narrative accounts by saying that these reports show us, through the real-life experiences of real people, that the unbearable can be borne, and has been borne, by many people living under extreme duress.[20]

Today, more and more people are telling the story of their journey through life after finding themselves with an incurable illness. These personal accounts of success and failure on the way to their gradual admission and acceptance of their particular disability contain a great deal of self-revelatory material that is not usually discussed in ordinary conversation. For most authors, the primary goal in revealing such intimate experiences is to give hope and courage to other people suffering from similar illnesses. But in doing this, most writers are well aware that they also receive help to continue their struggle to live a day at a time under trying circumstances.

The self-care movement

How some people successfully cope with chronic illness involves still another critical factor, called self-care. Most of the spiritual and psychological gains made by the people described by Kenney and others probably could not have been achieved without a high level of day-to-day self-care. When one thinks of the many nonprofessional yet significant personal caring activities required in chronic illness (like pre- and postoperative care, pre- and postradiation assistance, medication control for pain, and periodic psychological support or challenge), the significance of self-care is evident.

Self-care may include a variety of caring behaviors, ranging from self-medication, to self-administered primary medical care, to the behavioral management of any number of chronic diseases. The term is also sometimes used in the literature to include self-help group or mutual help group activities, which will be discussed later. In its most generic sense, self-care involves almost anything that people do for themselves to remain healthy or to treat illness or injury. Few people realize that self-care is the dominant form of medical care, accounting for 85 to 95 percent of all medical care. And, as Donald Vickery points out, even a small decrease in medical self-care for minor illnesses would cause an enormous increase in the number of doctor visits. For example,

Rottenberg estimated that if only two percent of individuals who use over-the-counter drugs for minor illnesses were to visit the doctor instead, the annual increase in office visits would be $292 million, a 62 percent rise.

Conversely, a small increase in the amount of medical self-care would cause a substantial decrease in professional visits for minor illnesses.[21]

The impact of self-care in chronic illness has perhaps even greater economic consequences, although there is little research in this area. Nevertheless, it is well known that much of the care involved in chronic illness is self-care. People with chronic illness and their significant others must take responsibility for a major portion of their care. And responsible physicians are continuing to recognize that the key to optimum management of chronic illness is effective self-care by the patient or care by other nonprofessionals.

Despite our knowledge that self-care is the dominant form of care in both acute and chronic illness, despite the growing trend toward enhancing personal decision making in health care, and despite the fact that public interest in self-care is rapidly expanding, the self-help movement is still limited by a number of issues.

Some of the unresolved issues in the self-care debate include the safety of self-care, its legal status, and its effectiveness; the reluctance of health promotion advocates to enter the medical care arena; inadequate professional reimbursement; inadequate funding for research; and where to draw the line between professional care and self-care, between quackery and legitimate self-care programs.[22]

There are ongoing debates in the United States and Europe about the social and political implications of health care reforms that advocate more self-care. Some critics caution that the trend toward increased emphasis on preventive health education and self-care could act as an excuse to cut back on a variety of public services to the poor. They fear that focusing on individual lifestyle changes without first dealing with the social conditions that bring about both poverty and disease would be misleading and unfair. The main concern is that massive government attempts to make people responsible for their own health may divert public attention from needed government efforts to modify a variety of social, political, and economic factors that also negatively affect the health of millions of people. Stokes does not believe this concern is justified:

> Does one try to change the social and economic system first, or change people first? Is lung cancer the result of a personal decision to smoke, or is it caused by the stress of

modern life and the advertising that encourages people to smoke? Clearly, society should do more to curb the power of tobacco companies to promote an unhealthy habit, but millions of Americans have quit smoking without drastic changes in the system. People can begin to alter their fates through activities that are not overtly political.[23]

In spite of the absence of substantial research on the effectiveness of medical self-care education and the social and political implications of the increased use of self-care, the fact remains that the potential for self-care to provide major health-enhancing benefits and to reduce health care costs to people with chronic illness is so enormous and the need so great that the self-care movement will continue to expand. And part of that growth will take place because of a closely related aspect of self-care called the self-help group movement, or, interchangeably or alternatively, the mutual help group movement.

The self-help group movement

An even more extensive source of evidence that chronically ill people can improve their health care situation is contained in the growing body of literature on the self-help, or mutual help, group movement. This movement, as it relates to chronic illness, dates from the founding of Alcoholics Anonymous (AA) in 1935.[24] Many of these groups are modeled after AA as it is described in what is commonly called "the Big Book." The person with the chronic problem is encouraged to become part of the solution by getting together with other people who share the same problem. Today, an estimated six million to fifteen million people belong to some five hundred thousand local self-help groups in the United States alone.[25] Whatever the exact number, most investigators are confident that self-help groups will assume a central role in the nation's physical and mental health care delivery system over the next two decades.[26]

These groups may be classified in different ways. There are groups for almost every kind of chronic physical or mental illness: there are recovery groups for people with problems such as alcoholism, drug addiction, or other compulsive or addictive behaviors (e.g., gambling, sex), and there are groups for people with certain kinds of socially stigmatizing handicaps (e.g., short/tall stature, facial disfigurement). . . .

Space does not permit a listing of all the self-help groups in the country. However, a review of the literature clearly demonstrates their similar basic concepts, common characteristics, and fundamental human wisdom. Some of these helping/caring characteristics are listed below:

1. The same people who provide the services consume the services and

2. They serve an unmet need—the need for mutual aid for special chronic problems.
3. The goal is to improve the psychological functioning, quality of life, and effectiveness in living for the individual members and the group itself.
4. Participation is voluntary, face-to-face, and in small groups. Large conferences may be held periodically.
5. The major source of help resides in the members' combined efforts and skills, their mutual experiences, and their understanding and concern for each other.
6. Self-help groups tend to be directly helpful, productive, inexpensive, nonbureaucratic, nonprofessional, and subjective (rather than objective) in relationships.
7. They provide multiple opportunities for members to experience mutual caring, altruism, and psychological growth.
8. They represent a new kind of group therapy, one based on the wisdom of the group, not on the authority of a professional group leader.
9. In such peer groups, as O. H. Mowrer pointed out, members meet as equals, sharing a common chronic problem. Under these circumstances, they tend to practice honest self-revelation, at least about their common problems. As a result of this experience, members modify some of their values and attitudes and frequently report enjoying improved mental health.[27]

The fundamental wisdom of experience communicated directly or indirectly in many of these self-help groups appears to be modeled after the basic wisdom of Alcoholics Anonymous and its Twelve Step program. . . .

While AA-oriented, Twelve Step groups are still the fastest growing and largest segment of the mutual help group movement. Other groups that do not directly identify with AA philosophy are growing too, with a similar focus on personal mutual caring and concern. *The Self-Help Sourcebook* offers a national listing of most of these groups.[28] Still other groups focus primarily on political action, seeking personal rights or direct empowerment for a number of disadvantaged groups. Examples would include the Disabled Rights movement, Mothers Against Drunk Driving, Parents of Retarded Children, Families of the Mentally Ill, and gay groups. As Frank Riessman, the Director of the National Self-Help Clearinghouse in New York City has pointed out, "These groups focus on and have effectively altered legislation, changed practices, influenced the schools, the medical profession and the media."[29]

Appendix 2

The question arises, If you have a chronic, somewhat incapacitating disorder or if you are living with a person with such a condition, should you join a mutual help group? As the movement grows, and as more groups are formed to deal with more kinds of chronic conditions, the answer becomes increasingly positive. Self-help groups are effective, and more and more chronic illnesses are being included in the movement.[30] But it should be remembered that the movement is still new. With the exception of AA and Al-Anon (a selfhelp group for the family members of the alcoholic),[31] it still faces a multitude of very ordinary growth problems, particularly since most groups emerge out of the multiple demoralizing experiences of people with chronic problems. Thus it takes time, experience, and a great deal of mutual soul-searching for some groups to get organized and focused enough to be truly effective in providing caring services for their members.[32]

For example, all mutual help groups must deal with several issues:

- leadership
- organization
- development
- financial needs
- networking with people who need their services
- other organizations
- maintaining confidentiality
- providing a mutually helpful and cooperative ongoing program of caring and concern

Nevertheless, the expectations for the future are that more and more people with chronic illness will share in the growth and development of mutual help groups.

John Naisbitt, in his best-selling book on the ten political, societal, and economic trends that will shape our future, lists the movement away from institutional help to self-help as one of the megatrends taking place in America today. He is convinced that the growth of the self-help movement is assured because "in a sense, we have come full circle. We are reclaiming America's traditional sense of self-reliance after four decades of trusting in institutional help."[33]

And support for the movement is coming from a number of powerful directions besides the people needing help. Former Surgeon General C. Everett Koop, for example, sponsored a workshop on self-help and public health in September of 1987. He expressed his concern there with the statement:

> I believe in self-help as an effective way of dealing with problems, stress, hardship, and pain. . . . Mending people, curing them, is no longer enough; it is only part of the total health care that most people require.[34]

About two hundred guests attended the workshop, most of them representing some self-help or mutual help group. Their charge was to develop recommendations that the Surgeon General could help to implement through the U.S. Public Health Service. The results of the workshop, the recommendations made, and the comments by Dr. Koop can be found in the proceedings published by the Public Health Service.[35]

One of the major goals of the Surgeon General's workshop was to encourage healthcare providers to become better acquainted with the various services offered by mutual help groups and to work more closely with these groups. Attempts to develop such partnerships are being made on a number of fronts, as the following examples will illustrate.

A symposium on the impact of life-threatening conditions and how self-help groups and health care providers can work in partnership to cope with such conditions was held in Chicago, Illinois, in the spring of 1989. The six sponsors of the symposium already represented a dynamic partnership: the Illinois Self-Help Center, the Foundation of Thanatology, the American Medical Association, the University of Illinois at Chicago School of Public Health, the U.S. Administration on Aging, and the American Association of Retired Persons. Some of the chronic disabilities discussed were death and dying, human immunodeficiency virus (HIV), cancer, physical disabilities, mental health, bereavement, the caregivers of older Americans, and adolescents with chronic conditions. A wide variety of workable ideas emerged for modifying and transforming the relationship between health care providers and self-help groups.[36]

Another significant attempt to develop a partnership is the National Project for Self-Help Groups at George Mason University in Fairfax, Virginia. The project is supported by a grant from the Office of Maternal and Child Health, under the aegis of the U.S. Department of Health and Human Services. The focus of the project is to increase both public and professional awareness of the concept, uses, and benefits of self-help groups. Attempts are being made to provide better collaboration between health professionals, researchers, self-help clearinghouses, public agencies, and mutual help groups through diverse networking strategies. It is especially important that one of the goals of the project be to develop an educational model for health care providers and public health agencies. Part of the emphasis here will be on the development of self-help models for young people.[37]

Appendix 2

Coping with chronic illness: a role/resource collaboration model

From the foregoing description of some of the organizational and communication problems that exist in mutual help groups—as well as between these groups and professional health care providers—it should be evident that comprehensive health care services for chronically ill people and their families are still very limited. Evaluated systematically, the major limitations that exist within each level of care—professional care, self-care, and self-help groups—are readily apparent.

Professional health care

The limitations in professional health care are primarily due to the contemporary structure of the caregiving model. The model is still based on an acute-illness, episodic-intervention, fee-for-service format rather than one more suitable for coping with a chronic illness. Not only are there structural limitations, but human limitations as well. Health care professionals continue to be trained to treat and cure both medical diseases and psychiatric disorders, but not to attend to other quality-of-life factors that are unique to chronic illness. Thus few health care professionals are trained (or can be reimbursed) for helping chronically ill patients cope with a variety of other problems that usually accompany chronic conditions. (Those that are trained offer a very limited range of services.) Gillick points out that this state of affairs is in itself a chronic condition, at least for physicians:

> The essential features of chronicity remain unchanged: incurability, inexorable decline and a slow rate of change in clinical symptoms. Similarly, many of the essential attributes of physicians remain unchanged: they are trained to thrive on cure; if not cure, at least improvement, and if not improvement, then rapid change in clinical course.[38]

Perhaps the best current description of the multiple conflicts facing the physician in coping with a chronically ill patient is that presented by Kleinman in *The Illness Narratives*.[39] He is well aware that what the physician in our contemporary Western culture treats as disease often has little to do with what the patient experiences as illness. His basic argument is that technological advances have changed the practice of medicine in ways that make it less helpful. He believes that interpreting the illness experience to the patient ought to be the core of medical training, when in fact, it is tragically neglected.

What should be done to improve the care of the chronically ill? Kleinman holds that the development of a biopsychosocial model of health care would better bridge the gap between patient and practitioner. Such an expanded model would in turn humanize a health care system that has lost touch with the patient.[40]

The health care situation is even more demoralizing when one turns to the care of the chronically mentally ill. There appears to be a reluctance on the part of all concerned to provide adequate, humane care. According to Shadish:

> Two profit-making industries, nursing homes and board-and-care homes, care for about one million chronic mental patients. This care is primarily custodial and probably not very different from the care patients received in the public sector prior to deinstitutionalization. Moreover, certain characteristics of privately owned facilities encourage poor patient care so as to maximize profit. The problem could be ameliorated if chronic mental patients were strong and informed consumers or if the public sector strongly regulated propriety care. However, neither of these two conditions now holds. Perhaps the apparent difficulties in significantly improving care for chronically mentally ill individuals despite seemingly major changes in policy reflect a fundamental problem in overall social policy—a reluctance to care for chronically indigent individuals of all kinds.[41]

Shadish offers little hope for immediate help with this pervasive problem. His main reason for taking this position is his belief that we do not want to take the necessary economic, political, and social steps to improve the condition of chronic mental patients because we have always viewed them as one part of an amorphous class of chronically indigent people "whom we do not value and would just as soon ignore."[42] His only hope is that research may lead to an understanding of

> the processes that give rise to the social, political, and economic problems of chronic mental patients, the institutional structures that contribute to the origin and persistence of these problems, the social arrangements that overwhelm efforts to eradicate them, and the points at which they are vulnerable to societal intervention. . . .[43]

The problems that arise most frequently in the professional health care sector have to do with the high level of public expectation of the curative powers of medicine. Yet at the same time, very slow progress is being made in modifying chronic illness. At the same time, the needs of the chronically ill go well beyond ordinary fee-for service medical and psychiatric treatment schedules. Obviously, a more holistic approach is needed, one that is more patient-oriented, one that makes more use of interdisciplinary treatment teams, and one that assumes greater responsibility in monitoring patient self-care. Despite remarkable technological advances, professional health care has, without question, serious limitations.[44]

Self-care

Self-care means taking care of oneself by following prescribed medication, dietary, or therapeutic regimens. While self-care plays an increasingly crucial role in coping with chronic illness, it too has serious limitations. One of the major issues, as has been pointed out by several investigators, has to do with a certain professional ambiguity about the value of self-care. Can a layperson really perform medical and psychological tasks adequately? How effective are the self-care practices now in use? The evidence is still meager and the area in need of more research (although the research that is available is positive). People will practice self-care, even complex procedures, it seems, if they are properly instructed and monitored. Thus self-care that emerges from an affiliation with a mutual help group or from various forms of professional health care education can have a significant impact on improving the quality of life for people with all kinds of illnesses and can dramatically cut hospital and medical costs.[45]

But health care education and patient compliance with that education continue to be problematic. Recent studies indicate that regardless of what condition one observes—chronic pain, diabetes, schizophrenia, hyperactivity in children, bipolar affective disorder, nicotine addiction—up to 50 percent of patients either would not or could not follow the advice of their health care advisors.[46] With such noncompliance rates, it is no wonder that health care professionals become pessimistic about the ability of patients to practice self-care.

There are some potential solutions to this patient noncompliance problem, however. One has to do with the need for improving information and education about patients' health care needs. To demonstrate this need, Searle pharmaceutical company, maker of a variety of drugs for hypertension, conducted a survey which indicated that nearly half of the patients using their preparations did not follow the dosage instructions of their medicine. They responded by voluntarily modifying all of their patient instruction sheets so that physicians could give their patients clearer, more easily understood information about the hypertensive drug they were taking, such as its side effects and interactions with other drugs, in straightforward, nontechnical terms.[47]

Meichenbaum and Turk, on the other hand, are finding that the relationship between the health care practitioner and the patient is a significant determining factor in patient compliance. They believe that a variety of special techniques can be developed to ensure greater patient compliance, such as the willingness of the practitioner to (a) monitor and assess the degree of noncompliance and (b) apply a number of strategies and procedures that are likely to facilitate compliance.[48] The difficulty here is that in order to facilitate patient compliance, health care practitioners must learn to modify much of their by-now stereotyped and streamlined office procedures and to communicate much more openly and directly with their patients about their illness.

The self-help group movement

Even the most rapidly growing and most extensive form of structured self-care is of limited use in coping with chronic illness. On one hand, people with chronic physical and emotional illnesses can help themselves by helping each other. On the other hand, self-help groups are not formal social service organizations. Especially in their fledgling stage, they are very fragile and small groups of fellow sufferers who are just trying to live one day at a time with a chronic illness. The major deficiency may be that self-help groups need a good deal of time to mature in their wisdom and philosophy for coping with specific illnesses. And then the growing groups need time to bring this message of wisdom, experience, and caring to other people in need, who in turn start other new groups. As Stokes has noted, this movement is still in its infancy and has many powerful cultural, institutional, and bureaucratic forces to overcome before its experiential learning can be freely communicated.[49]

What can be done in the face of all of these limitations? Or is there a better way to do whatever it is that needs to be done? Despite the limitations inherent in each aspect of care (professional, self-care, and self-help groups), each is still needed if we are even to begin to cope with chronic illness more effectively, more humanely, and more efficiently. Is it possible that some kind of rapprochement can be developed? It seems we need a combination of forces, all of which are able to act in a concerted effort to bring about the highest level of coping and the optimum response possible in any given patient with any given chronic illness.

This kind of collaborative interaction has been described in a more circumscribed fashion by Tyler et al. with respect to the psychologist-client interaction. The point made here is that despite limitations, most traditional professional helping situations use a unidirectional influence model; that is, the expert helper tries to understand and influence the client. This model creates a paradoxical situation, however, since it creates a basic incongruity. Despite the fact that the expert helper is trying to foster client independence, the unidirectional relationship actually fosters

Appendix 2

dependence. Consequently, an alternative helping model that would emphasize collaboration and mutual exchange has been proposed. Called the "resource collaboration model," the goal is to develop expert-nonexpert relationships that involve reciprocal interactions wherein "all participants acknowledge their own and each other's resources and limitations, share their resources, and recognize their reciprocal gains."[50]

In his final chapter on the care of the chronically ill, Kleinman explains that the new kind of physician will be a medical psychotherapist who can skillfully develop a clinical methodology in which the patient, family, and physician relationships become flexible collaborations.[51]

Even though the resource collaboration model is not yet in full bloom, there are a few fascinating examples in the literature that illustrate collaborative interactions between professionals, patients with various chronic illnesses, and significant others. Most of the studies represent experimental research projects; nevertheless, it seems possible to use these models to work more collaboratively with patients living with chronic illnesses.

Mental illness

Perhaps it should first be emphasized that a great variety of chronic behavioral disorders profoundly disrupt the lives of millions of people in the United States each year. These disorders include both childhood and adult mental illnesses, such as schizophrenia, affective disorders, Alzheimer's disease, anxiety disorders, personality disorders, learning disabilities, eating disorders, and so forth. In addition, there are millions of adolescents and adults who have one or another form of alcohol or drug abuse. Almost thirty million Americans may suffer from alcohol abuse, other drug abuse, or mental disorders at any given time, causing much morbidity and mortality.[52] The total direct and indirect costs for alcohol abuse, other drug abuse, and mental disorders in the United States are now estimated to be around $273.3 billion a year. These latest figures, published by the Alcohol, Drug Abuse and Mental Health Administration in 1990 and using updated costs from 1988 estimates, place mental illness as the costliest disorder at $129.3 billion, followed by $85.8 billion for alcohol abuse and $58.3 billion for drug abuse.[53]

While most of these conditions involve highly complex causal interactions that require expert professional help, there is growing recognition that a number of behavioral and emotional components of care can be handled with the help of paraprofessionals, family members, and the patients themselves. The continued growth of mutual help group organizations like Recovery, Inc., Emotions Anonymous, National Alliance for the Mentally Ill, Schizophrenics Anonymous, Association for Retarded Citizens, and the like, all support the idea that collaborative efforts work best in chronic mental illness.[54] It is apparent that such a movement must make extensive use of noninstitutional and nonprofessional services, including paraprofessional mental health workers, patient self-help groups, group homes, and a variety of structured self-help programs for family members.

Schizophrenia. Of all the mental illnesses, this debilitating disorder affecting about two million Americans is by far the most devastating, since it readily produces chronic disability and impaired function. Yet Stokes, in reviewing this literature, points out that

> case studies show that the rehospitalization rate of chronic schizophrenics who were treated by non-professional community networks was cut in half, and those who were rehospitalized spent less time back in the institutions than schizophrenics who were treated by formal mental health agencies.
>
> The medical establishment is beginning to recognize that people with chronic diseases can often do much to take care of themselves. Organized self-care programs, often staffed by people who suffer from the same illness and with whom patients can easily identify, are proving to be successful and cost-effective replacements for professional medical supervision.[55]

Perhaps the most compelling argument about the impact of self-care on the course of schizophrenia is found in the research literature that investigates the behavior of relatives of schizophrenics. These studies came about partly because of the movement towards deinstitutionalization, which took place in the 1960s and which meant that thousands of schizophrenic patients would be discharged from mental hospitals and returned home to live with their families or friends. The research seems to offer convincing evidence that family interaction is directly relevant to the course of schizophrenia and that a modification of family behavior is especially helpful in preventing relapse.[56]

The literature on intervention with families of schizophrenics has recently been reviewed by Rohrbaugh. After examining a number of controlled studies, he concluded that when client-based professional care was compared with a family approach (consisting mainly of education and behavior management training for the relatives), the family approach was clearly superior to the individual approach in preventing rehospitalization, improving medication compliance, and reducing symptoms over a nine- to twelve-month period.[57]

The Harvard Medical School Mental Health Letter of June 1989 summarized the history and present studies on the value of involving families in the treatment of schizophrenia and reached conclusions similar to those of Rohrbaugh. Despite some methodological limitations, recent studies comparing traditional client-focused professional care with treatment programs that also included a family education and training component show that programs with a family involvement sequence have lower patient-relapse rates along with better patient-family compatibility reports. There is need for continued research, of course, as well as for the development of a more balanced perspective on the role of the family in schizophrenia. The article concludes: "Having learned that the family is not the main problem in schizophrenia, we must not act as though it is the main solution."[58]

Asthma

This is another extensive chronic condition that can be much better controlled with an appropriate self-care program. In one large study conducted by the National Heart, Lung and Blood Institute, children in several experimental asthma self-management programs showed significant improvement in terms of presentation and management of asthma attacks, fewer school days lost, and reduced hospital and medical costs. In one program, asthmatic children lost an average of eleven fewer school days in the year following the program. In another study, hospital costs and emergency room visits were reduced by an average of $943 per year—a savings of $11.50 for every dollar spent on the program. In an article describing these programs, Sydney Parker, program administrator for the studies, is quoted as saying that

> asthma is the leading cause of chronic illness and school absenteeism in children under 17.... The economic impact of asthma self-management on reducing hospitalizations and emergency-room visits alone can save millions of dollars in health-care costs....[59]

Of course, using self-management techniques in these programs as well as focusing on personal responsibility for health care in no way detracts from the need for patients to maintain an effective, ongoing partnership with their physicians.

Diabetes mellitus

This is perhaps the best example of a chronic physical illness that must be monitored and treated through patient self-care. Structured diabetes classes are now offered at many clinics and hospitals. Patient education appears to be improved when classes offer both information and the stimulus of group support and shared experiences. With respect to cost containment in diabetes, Stokes reports that

> a self-care program for diabetics run by the University

of Southern California Medical Center . . . reduced the number of patients experiencing diabetic coma by two-thirds, and saved hospitals and patients $1.4 million over a two-year period.[60]

The successful treatment of diabetes depends entirely on how well the patient can modify and control his or her blood sugar level through medication, diet, exercise, and stress level. Consequently, the teaching of self-care and the periodic monitoring of compliance are of crucial importance in controlling this essentially behavioral illness.[61]

Chronic pain

Various forms of acute and chronic pain are considered the most widespread type of distress experienced by human beings. The personal, social, and economic costs of pain and attempts at pain control are staggering. Kleinman has recently commented on this fact:

> Almost all of us will suffer some significant pain in our lives, and at least half of us will have serious [incapacitating] pain. Several studies in North America find a prevalence of serious pain complaints ranging from 7 to 18 percent of the population in the course of a year. One survey indicated that 1 in 7 Americans have chronic back pain and 1 in 10 have chronic muscle pain. Of all visits to physicians recorded in the National Ambulatory Medical Care Survey, almost 3 percent were for back pain. In a British study, back pain caused work absences of at least 21 days among 15 percent of miners. A study in Quebec shows that backpain becomes chronic in about 8 percent of workers who develop it.[62]

Kleinman goes on to say that although there is no evidence for the existence of a "pain-prone personality," we know very little about the kinds of people who become chronic pain patients. In severe cases of chronic pain, he recommends an overall psychosocial approach to treatment using multidisciplinary programs.

Turk et al. have also reviewed the literature of chronic pain, especially the more recent attempts to control pain by using a variety of cognitive-behavioral approaches. In their practical guide to the issues involved in pain management, the authors' central focus appears to be on the need for a collaborative interaction between the patient, the family members living in significant relationships with the patient, and the health care professionals involved. In order to bring about improved pain control, we must address multiple interacting factors: patient motivation, adherence to treatment regime, ongoing maintenance of treatment effects, the patient therapist relationship, and the role of the patient's significant others. Group treatment is also found to be as effective as individual therapy, and group cognitive-behavioral treatment can be flexibly combined with individual, couple, or family therapy sessions.

While Turk et al. carefully avoid presenting their research as a panacea, they are nevertheless enthusiastic about applying these techniques both to pain control and to a wide variety of other health promotion, disease prevention, and disease treatment problems.[63]

Hospice movement

This rapidly growing organization represents another example of an apparently fruitful blending of professional care, self-help, and self-help group collaboration. In this sense, the hospice movement represents an alternative way of dealing with death and dying. By definition the hospice movement focuses on the treatment of the terminally ill by providing care in the last phase of incurable disease. The goal is to help the terminally ill to live as fully and comfortably as possible. It is not only the trained professional staff members who provide care, but also the volunteers, patients, and family members who participate in and partake of the caregiving.

The hospice movement is really a self-help group in terms of origin and development. Like other self-help groups, it started growing and continues to grow because of a specific human need that society could not provide. Its goal was to develop a more appropriate form of terminal care than was being provided by the prevailing technological and often dehumanizing model, which focused on frequently costly and inappropriate acute care—that is, cure-oriented approaches.[64]

Alcoholism

A growing body of research is demonstrating that the practice of self-care and mutual help group affiliation helps many people with chronic physical or mental illnesses to improve the quality of their lives. The report of the Surgeon General's Workshop on Self-Help and Public Health previously mentioned lists positive outcomes in controlled studies for people with emphysema, chronic bronchitis or asthma, women with metastatic breast cancer, people with rheumatoid arthritis, and mental patients discharged from two state hospital programs.[65] However, the helping networks being developed for these as well as other chronic conditions do not seem to be as well structured as those found in some of the contemporary programs developed to treat alcoholism. The following is a brief description of one of the major ways of intervening in alcoholism, a chronic illness still socially rejected and once considered hopeless.

In the United States there are an estimated 10.6 million alcoholics and 7.3 million alcohol abusers in the adult population (eighteen years and older). Fifteen to 18 percent of the population will exhibit a dependence problem with alcohol or other drugs at some time during their lifetime. The 10 percent of drinkers (6.5 percent of the total adult population) who drink the most heavily account for half of all the alcohol consumed, with the other half accounted for by the remaining 90 percent, who are infrequent, light, or moderate drinkers. An estimated 4.6 million adolescents between the ages of fourteen and seventeen experience negative consequences from alcohol use.[66] Alcohol abuse and alcoholism cost the nation $85.8 billion a year in direct and indirect costs.[67]

Despite centuries of concern, few communities have developed helpful and cost-effective responses to the illness of alcoholism. Yet as Fein and others have pointed out, treatment for alcoholism is cost-effective and can result in subsequent reductions in treatment for other health disorders.[68]

Without question, untreated alcoholism is closely associated with a variety of other illnesses that require high-cost hospitalization. Zook and Moore found that a comparatively small fraction of hospital patients (about 13 percent) used more than half of the hospital resources in a year.[69] Most of these high-cost patients suffered from alcoholism, smoked too much, and were overweight. In a follow-up study, Zook, Zavickis, and Moore found the typical high-cost patient experienced multiple hospitalizations for the same disease. Most significantly, patients with a history of chronic alcoholism had a much higher incidence of repeated hospitalizations than patients with no alcoholism in their background.[70]

Although limited by cost considerations, alcoholism treatment has become increasingly multimodal and multidisciplinary. It is generally recognized that a comprehensive system of essential services is necessary if the various physical, psychological, social, and spiritual needs of the alcoholic are to be treated successfully. Because of the growing professional awareness of the multiple factors involved in the development and progression of illness, a remarkable role-resource collaboration model of treatment has been in the process of rapid growth and refinement in the United States over the past twenty years. It has been estimated that the majority of the treatment centers in the United States are based on such a comprehensive model.[71]

The basic assumption underlying this treatment model is that alcoholism is a chronic, primary, usually progressive illness that requires a caring rather than a curing philosophy of treatment. Alcoholism is considered a multidimensional illness, since numerous physical, psychological, social, and spiritual sequence are associated with it. Even though the illness cannot be cured, this model holds that it can be successfully arrested if most of the essential needs of the alcoholic and the family are met and if the client develops and adheres to an individualized, comprehensive care plan.[72]

Acute professional care for alcoholics and their families involves a range of services called a "continuum of care," which may include diagnostic and referral services, detoxification, short-term primary residential care, extended care, residential intermediate care (halfway houses), outpatient services, aftercare, and family services.

Since alcoholism is a multiphasic illness, a multidisciplinary staff provides selected professional services throughout these programs. Medical, nursing, psychiatric, psychological, social, and clinical pastoral services are provided by specially trained professionals. However, the vast majority of the day-to-day direct, individual, small-group, and self-care educational services are delivered by trained (and usually certified) alcoholism counselors who have recovered from alcoholism themselves or who have had considerable experience living with alcoholism in their families.

The fundamental goal in alcoholism treatment is to help the patient and significant others learn to make certain necessary, and sometimes major, lifestyle changes that will help them live and cope successfully with an incurable illness. In order to do this, the patient is taught to be highly involved in certain self-care and self-help group practices that will ensure a lasting and satisfactory sobriety, such as by participating in a prescriptive aftercare plan and attending Alcoholics Anonymous meetings regularly.

Most comprehensive alcoholism treatment programs initiate these lifestyle changes by first helping alcoholic patients to admit that they are in fact unable to regulate their use of alcohol or some other mind-altering substance consistently. Because of this loss of control—this involuntary chronic disability—their lives are, to that extent, unmanageable. This phase of treatment—to help alcoholic patients admit and accept that they do have a chronic illness that can no longer be denied—must be dealt with first before further progress can be made.

Throughout the whole treatment process, patients are treated with dignity and respect, and most services are structured so clients can take an appropriate degree of personal responsibility for making necessary behavioral changes. Many patient activities involve meeting in structured or unstructured peer groups, with and without professional supervision. In such situations, patients learn to help themselves by helping each other. They also learn that when fellow sufferers join together to share common chronic problems, remarkable positive attitudinal and behavioral changes take place.

The test of any treatment program, of course, is its degree of effectiveness. Despite multiple problems of measurement in this complex area, an increasing number of positive and consistent patient-outcome estimates based on this model are available.[73]

Alcoholism as metaphor

In reviewing the literature on how various chronic disabilities affect people, we see that alcoholism appears to represent almost all the critical conditions that make for human limitation and suffering. Without question, alcoholism is a chronic condition: it is multidimensional; it is disabling; it is unpredictable; there is no possibility of cure; the illness determines one's lifestyle; the causes and symptoms are ambiguous and unpredictable; there is shame and guilt; there is obvious loss of control; and certainly most alcoholics and family members feel as if they were bearing the unbearable much of the time.

Alcoholism is also similar to other chronic illnesses in terms of psychological response—how one bears the unbearable. Although some alcoholics respond to the condition of alcoholism heroically, many others do not. Rather, like other chronically ill people, they ignore the symptoms, incorrectly diagnose themselves, delay seeking professional care, seek help only in a crisis, and then want only symptomatic treatment. They deny the chronicity of the illness, reject professional advice, minimize or rationalize their condition, or react to their alcoholism, as Schuckit has pointed out, with a "bewildering array" of distressing emotional and behavioral responses.[74]

The psychological responses of significant others living with an alcoholic are also similar to those of significant others living with loved ones who suffer from other chronic illnesses. Not only can these significant others respond to the sufferer's condition with an array of disturbing emotions, but all too frequently they can also become demoralized if they believe that they must give up their wants and needs and live primarily for the sometimes-excessive demands made by the person with the chronic illness. Over the past few years, the growing realization that family members of practicing alcoholics, as well as caretakers of other persons with chronic conditions, need help for themselves under these stressful circumstances has been addressed in a variety of educational materials and self-help organizations designed to help the helpers.[75]

The basic therapeutic generalization implied in all of this is that for any patient, family member, or significant other living with a debilitating chronic illness, the whole tragic situation can become more bearable. Psychological and social healing can take place to the extent that each involved person can do the following:

1. Turn denial and rationalization of the condition into admission and acceptance.
2. Affiliate with a mutual help group coping with a similar chronic illness.
3. Practice some kind of recommended daily self-care.

Strange and paradoxical as it may seem, for those who are able to take these basic steps, living with a chronic illness can become a therapeutically transcending experience—one can bear the unbearable. In this larger sense, alcoholism and our improved methods of coping with it may well be a metaphor for coping with many other devastating chronic illnesses.

Discussion

For most of us living in the developed nations of the world, surviving an acute illness is becoming increasingly common. However, while more effective physical and psychological care enables us to live longer, the increasing prevalence of chronic illness means that living longer also involves living a life in which a proportionately longer period is spent in chronic ill health. Some health care professionals are becoming concerned about the inevitable unmet health care needs.[76] Callahan put it well in an article discussing the ethical problems associated with escalating health care costs, euthanasia, and chronic illness:

> Beyond the hospital setting there have been other important general trends. The broadest and most encompassing is the increase in chronic illness, particularly that ensuing upon acute episodes of life-saving interventions. More of those episodes are followed by a long decline toward death often marked by sporadic acute recurrences where the patient is brought through once again. An increase in the time between the determination of a terminal illness or fatal disease and death is still another important change, now reaching three years in the case of cancer deaths. An extended life with a chronic illness, and an extended dying, are growing consequences of improved medical care.[77]

Despite the multiple complex issues involved, a number of ideas and partial solutions come to mind, ranging from modifying health insurance programs to increasing the funding for research studies of chronic illness. As a matter of practical humanitarian need, a small number of concerned health care professionals have altered their perspective on health care from the predominant acute illness model (fee-for-service, episodic intervention, be-cured-or-die) to one more in keeping with coping with chronic illness. The focus is on maintaining the patient's quality of life, instructing the patient in self-care procedures, and providing long-term support of a person who may live with the illness for an extended period of time. But the present health care fee-for-service reimbursement system designed for acute illness does little to support this alternative approach to treatment.[78]

Because most of the pioneer work being done in the area of chronic illness is relatively uncoordinated and frequently uncommunicated to other service providers, one of the great needs is to bring the existing helping forces together for future workshops and strategy meetings similar to the Surgeon General's Workshop on Self-Help and Public Health. Another major issue we need to address—and perhaps the most primary one—is to develop a better description of the phenomenon of chronic illness as a discrete and identifiable process with distinct commonalities of necessary coping and caring practices. What we need is a general taxonomy of the major variables of the experience. What does it mean to all of the people involved—the person with chronic illness, family members, professional caregivers—to be rather suddenly confronted with a condition involving irrevocable loss? What are the common reactions of these people to the significant events that usually take place in chronic illness—events like the discovery process associated with the specific chronic condition, the ensuing experience of irrevocable loss, the associated grief process and its fluctuations, the experience of giving and receiving not temporary but long-term care, and the various treatment processes and medication effects? What about the impact of modification of individual roles and role relationships or the catastrophic economic dimensions? All of these elements of chronic illness need greater clarification and understanding if we are to face them more effectively and more humanely.

Another way of dealing more appropriately with the chronically ill is to understand the profound attitudinal differences that distinguish a caring from a curing point of view and to see how these different perspectives influence the roles played by all concerned. For example, in acute illness, the experiences of giving and receiving care and support are usually secondary to the short-term professional and technological activities of curing the person. In chronic illness, as important as the professional and technological activities may be, the major emphasis must necessarily be on long-term caring. But how skilled are we at caring? Do we really want to be that involved? Paraphrasing and summarizing some of Nouwen's comments, it seems that the basic meaning of caring is to grieve, to experience sorrow, to cry out with empathy. It seems that caring is not a relationship of the strong to the weak or the powerful to the powerless. When we ask ourselves which people in our lives mean the most to us, we often find it is those who share our pain and touch our wounds with a gentle and tender hand instead of those who may give advice, solutions, or cures.[79] Milton Mayeroff has also described the primacy and centrality of caring in terms of the human condition: "In the sense in which [one] can ever be said to be at home in the world, [one] is at home not through dominating, or explaining, or appreciating, but through caring and being cared for. . . ."[80]

But who teaches us how to care for ourselves or others when we are experiencing chronic illness? Yes, some experiential knowledge and wisdom are available, but they are communicated very informally and unsystematically. Very likely each particular chronic condition has its own specific and significant caring needs; thus this wisdom of experience needs to be shared more widely.

One of the reasons I have so much faith in the possibility that we can do a better job of helping people live with chronic illness comes from my own personal experience in working with recovering alcoholics and their families. There are hundreds of thousands of sober and reasonably happy recovering alcoholics living the program of Alcoholics Anonymous, along with spouses who are members of Al-Anon. All of these people have experienced the tragedy of living with a chronic illness, and some have failed to cope with it from time to time. Yet for most of them, coming to realize they can live with a chronic illness, learning they can modify lifestyles, learning they can cope with the realities of the day, becomes satisfying and rewarding in itself.

Something else also happens to many of them once they have faced up to and met the challenge of alcoholism: they are now more ready to meet other challenges in life. I call this new attitude, which grew out of the need to face up to a chronic illness, a "health maintenance attitude," because it seeks to restore and repair. It is also a health promotion attitude, since these people really want to stay well.

When people begin to face up to and live with their chronic condition, they become health maintenance advocates—not in spite of their condition but because of it. And the basic support and challenge to do this seem to come right out of the self-care, self-help group movement. Paradoxical as it may seem, an appropriate caring intervention into a late-stage chronic illness can lead some sick people to develop health maintenance living practices more associated with primary prevention. In fact, for some people, facing up to a chronic illness can lead to the primary prevention of any number of other disabling physical or psychological conditions.

Thus it is my impression that, for some people at least, chronic illness can be a transforming experience, even a new pathway to wholeness and health.

Endnotes

1. D. C. Taylor, "The Components of Sickness: Diseases, Illnesses, and Predicaments," *The Lancet* (10 November 1979): 1008-10.
2. A. Kleinman, *The Illness Narratives* (New York: Basic Books, 1988), 4–8.
3. B. Stokes, *Helping Ourselves: Local Solutions to Global Problems* (New York: Norton, 1981), 102.
4. D. C. Turk, D. Meichenbaum, and M. Genest, *Pain and Behavioral Medicine: A Cognitive-Behavioral Perspective* (New York: Guilford Press, 1983); J. D. Matarazzo, "Behavioral Health's Challenge to Academic, Scientific, and Professional Psychology," *American Psychologist* 37 (1982): 1–14.
5. "Trends in Medical Care Costs," *Metropolitan Life Statistical Bulletin* 70 (Jan.-Mar. 1989).
6. D. J. Cullen, L. C. Ferrara, B. A. Briggs, P. F. Walker, and J. Gilbert, "Survival, Hospitalization Charges and Follow-Up Results in Critically Ill Patients," *New England Journal of Medicine* (29 April 1976): 982–1309; P. T. Mengel, *Medical Costs, Moral Choices* (New Haven: Yale University Press, 1983); V. R. Fuchs, "Who Shall Live?" Health, Economics and Social Choice (New York: Basic Books, 1974).
7. Donald Vickery, M.D., President, Center for Corporate Health Promotion, Travelers Insurance Co., Reston, Va., personal communication, 11 September 1989.
8. K. Fisher, "Researchers Debate Lifestyle, Health Links," *APA Monitor* (December 1988): 12–14.
9. M. R. Gillick, "Is the Care of the Chronically Ill a Medical Prerogative?" *New England Journal of Medicine* 310 (19 January 1984): 190–93; T. G. Burish and L. A. Bradley, eds., *Coping with Chronic Disease: Research and Applications* (New York: Academic Press, 1983); M. C. Riddle, "A Strategy for Chronic Disease," *The Lancet* (4 October 1980): 734–36.
10. T. S. Szasz and M. H. Hollender, "A Contribution to the Philosophy of Medicine," *Archives of Internal Medicine* 87 (1956): 585-92, (referred to in Riddle, 1980).
11. Burish and Bradley, 9–13.
12. Lowell W. Levin, personal communication, Professor of Public Health, School of Medicine, Yale University, 12 September 1989.
13. L. E. Cluff, "Chronic Disease, Function and the Quality of Care," *Journal of Chronic Disease* 34 (1981): 299.
14. Burish and Bradley; Gillick; D. J. Feldman, "Chronic Disabling Illness: A Holistic View," *Journal of Chronic Disease* 27 (1974): 287–91.
15. The following are some of the sources that treat the subject of chronic illness. S. Breznitz, ed., *The Denial of Stress* (New York: International University Press, 1983); G. L. Bultena and E. A. Powers, "Denial of Aging: Age Identification and Reference Group Orientations," *Journal of Gerontology* 33, no. 5 (1978): 748–54; W. F. Baile and B. T. Engel, "A Behavioral Strategy for Promoting Treatment Compliance Following Myocardial Infarction," *Psychosomatic Medicine* 40 (August 1978); R. C. Casper, K. A. Halmi, S. C. Goldberg, E. D. Eckert, and J. M. Davis, "Disturbances in Body Image Estimation as Related to Other Characteristics and Outcome in Anorexia Nervosa," *British Journal of Psychiatry* 134 (1979): 60–66; Gliedman and Roth; T. P. Hackett and N. H. Cassem, "Development of a Quantitative Rating Scale to Assess Denial," *Journal of Psychosomatic Research* 18 (1974): 93–100; E. J. Kenney, Jr., "Death's Other Kingdom," *Commonweal* (19 November 1982): 627–32; E. Kurtz, *Not-God: A History of Alcoholics Anonymous* (Center City, Minn.: Hazelden Educational Materials, 1979); E. Kübler-Ross, *On Death and Dying* (New York: Macmillan, 1969); L. S. Levin and E. L. Idler, "Self-Care in Health," *Annual Review of Public Health* 4 (1983): 91–130; J. W. Vargo, "Some

Psychological Effects of Physical Disability," *American Journal of Occupational Therapy* 32 (January 1978): 31–34; C. J. Zook and F. D. Moore, "High-Cost Users of Medical Care," *New England Journal of Medicine* (1 May 1980); M. G. Eisenberg, L. C. Sutkin, and M. A. Jansen, eds., *Chronic Illness and Disability Through the Life Span: Effects on Self and Family* (New York: Springer Publishing Company, 1984); R. P. Marinelli and A. E. Dell Orto, *The Psychological and Social Impact of Physical Disability*, 2d ed. (New York: Behavioral Science Book Service, 1984).

16. Marinelli and Dell Orto, 1984; D. J. Huberty, "Adapting to Illness Through Family Groups," *International Journal of Psychiatry in Medicine* 5, no. 3 (1974): 231–42.
17. Kübler-Ross.
18. Kenney.
19. Kenney, 629.
20. Kenney, 632.
21. D. M. Vickery, "Medical Self-Care: A Review of the Concept and Program Models," *American Journal of Health Promotion* 1 (Summer 1986): 23–28.
22. Levin and Idler, 192; Vickery, 27.
23. Stokes, 105.
24. *Alcoholics Anonymous* [The Big Book] (New York: Alcoholics Anonymous World Services, 1955).
25. A. Gartner and F. Riessman, *The Self-Help Revolution* (New York: Human Sciences Press, 1982), 18; U.S. Department of Health and Human Services, *Promoting Health, Preventing Disease: Objectives for the Nation* (Washington, D.C.: U.S. Department of Health and Human Services, 1980); T. J. Powell, ed., *Working with Self-Help* (Silver Spring: National Association of Social Workers Press, 1989), vii.
26. M. K. Jacobs and G. Goodman, "Psychology and Self-Help Groups," *American Psychologist* 44 (March 1989): 536–45; U.S. Department of Health and Human Services, *The Surgeon General's Workshop on Self-Help and Public Health* (Washington: U.S. Government Printing Office, 1988).
27. O. H. Mowrer, *The New Group Therapy* (Princeton: Van Nostrand, 1964), iii–vi.
28. E. J. Madara and A. Meese, eds., *The Self-Help Sourcebook: Finding and Forming Mutual Aid Self-Help Groups*, 3d ed. (Denville, N.J.: Self-Help Clearinghouse, Saint Clares-Riverside Medical Center, 1990).
29. F. Riessman, *The Relationship of 12-Steppers to the Self-Help Movement* (draft), The National Self-Help Clearinghouse Graduate School and University Center/CUNY (September 1989).
30. "Effectiveness of Health Self-Help Groups," *Self-Help Reporter*, The National Self-Help Clearinghouse Graduate School and University Center/CUNY (winter/spring 1989); C. Cantor, "Support Groups Fill Emotional Gaps," *New York Times*, 28 September 1986: 1.
31. *Al-Anon Faces Alcoholism* (New York: Al-Anon Family Group Headquarters, 1965).
32. T. Powell, *Self-Help Organizations and Professional Practice* (Silver Spring: National Association of Social Workers Press, 1987); T. Powell, ed., *Working with Self-Help* (Silver Spring: National Association of Social Workers Press, 1990), 57–83.
33. J. Naisbirt, *Megatrends: Ten New Directions Transforming Our Lives* (New York: Warner Books, 1984), 143.
34. U.S. Department of Health and Human Services, Public Health Service, *The Surgeon General's Workshop on Self-Help and Public Health* (Washington, D.C.: U.S. Government Printing Office, 1988).
35. *The Surgeon General's Workshop on Self-Help and Public Health*.
36. American Medical Association, *The Impact of Life-Threatening Conditions: Self-Help Groups and Health Care Providers in Partnership* (Abstract), Chicago, 30 March–1 April 1989.
37. E. McGinn, Director, National Project

for Self-Help Groups, George Mason University, personal correspondence, October 1989.
38. Gillick, 190.
39. A. Kleinman, *The Illness Narratives* (New York: Basic Books, 1988), xiii.
40. Kleinman, 5–6.
41. W. R. Shadish, Jr., "Private-Sector Care for Chronically Ill Individuals; The More Things Change, the More They Stay the Same," *American Psychologist* 44 (August 1989): 1142.
42. Shadish, 1142.
43. Shadish, 1146.
44. Gillick; Cluff; E. Lefton and M. Lefton, "Health Care and Treatment for the Chronically Ill: Toward a Conceptual Framework," *Journal of Chronic Disease* 32 (1979): 339–44; A. T. Masi, "An Holistic Concept of Health and Illness: A Tricentermial Goal for Medicine and Public Health," *Journal of Chronic Disease* 31 (1978): 563–72; J. Buie, "Increase in Therapists Could Help Severely Ill," *APA Monitor* 20 (October 1989): 22.
45. D. M. Vickery et al., "Effect of a Self-Care Education Program on Medical Visits," *Journal of the American Medical Association* 250 (1983): 2952–56; Levin and Idler, 91–130; D. M. Vickery et al., "The Effects of Self-Care Interventions on the Use of Medical Services Within a Medicare Population," *Medical Care* 26 (June 1988), 580–88.
46. D. Meichenbaum and D. C. Turk, *Facilitating Treatment Adherence: A Practitioner's Guide* (New York: Behavioral Science Service, 1988), 12.
47. "Drugmaker Adopts Easily Understood Directions," *Minneapolis Star Tribune*, 21 October 1989: 2E.
48. Meichenbaum and Turk, 73.
49. Stokes; Weber and Dohen.
50. F. B. Tyler, K. I. Pargament, and M. Gatz, "The Resource Collaborator Role: A Model for Interactions Involving Psychologists," *American Psychologist* (April 1983): 388–98.
51. Kleinman, 229.
52. D. B. Kamerow et al., "Alcohol Abuse, Other Drug Abuse, and Mental Disorders in Medical Practice," *Journal of the American Medical Association* 255 (1986): 4.
53. U.S. Department of Health and Human Services, *Economic Costs of Alcohol and Drug Abuse and Mental Illness* (Washington, DC: GPO, 1985); Alcohol, Drug Abuse and Mental Health Administration (Rockville: National Clearinghouse for Alcohol and Drug Information, 1990).
54. The complete names, addresses, and telephone numbers of these as well as other mutual help group organizations may be found in E. Madara and A. Meese, eds., *The Self-Help Sourcebook: Finding and Forming Mutual Aid Self-Help Groups*, 3d ed. (Denville, N.J.: American Self-Help Clearinghouse, St. Clares-Riverside Medical Center, 1990).
55. Stokes, 102–3.
56. J. Leff, L. Kuipers, R. Berkowitz, R. Eberlein-Vries, and D. Sturgeon, "A Controlled Trial of Social Intervention in the Families of Schizophrenic Patients," *British Journal of Psychiatry* 141 (1982): 121–34; M. J. Goldstein and J. A. Doane, "Family Factors in the Onset, Course, and Treatment of Schizophrenic Spectrum Disorders," *Journal of Nervous and Mental Disease* 170, no. 11 (1982); C. Vaughn and J. Leff, "The Measurement of Expressed Emotion in the Families of Psychiatric Patients," *British Journal of Social Clinical Psychology* 15 (1976): 157–65.
57. M. Rohrbaugh, "Schizophrenia Research: Swimming Against the Mainstream," *Net-Worker* (July–August 1983).
58. "Families in the Treatment of Schizophrenia, Part I," *The Harvard Medical School Mental Health Letter* 5, no. 12 (1989): 1–4; Part II, 6, no. 1 (1989): 1–3.
59. "Asthmatic Kids Breathe Easier with Self-Help Aid," *USA Today*, 10 February 1984: 5D.
60. Stokes, 103.
61. C. Turkington, "Stress Found to Play

Appendix 2

Major Role in Onset, Treatment of Diabetes," *APA Monitor* 16 (February 1985): 28.

62. A. Kleinman, "Mental Health and Chronic Pain," *The Harvard Medical School Mental Health Letter* 6, no. 1 (1989): 4–5.
63. Turk et al., 64–69.
64. R.G. Benton, *Death and Dying: Principles and Practices in Patient Care* (New York: Van Nostrand Reinhold Company, 1978); A. Munley, *The Hospice Alternative: A New Context for Death and Dying* (New York: Basic Books, 1983), 272–73.
65. *The Surgeon General's Workshop on Self-Help and Public Health*, 272–73.
66. U.S. Department of Health and Human Services, *Sixth Special Report to the U.S. Congress on Alcohol and Health*, from the Secretary of Health and Human Services, January 1987. Also, *Seventh Special Report to the U.S. Congress on Alcohol and Health*, January 1990. Both reports are available from the National Clearinghouse for Alcohol and Drug Information, P.O. Box 2345, Rockville, MD 20852.
67. U.S. Department of Health and Human Services, *Economic Costs of Alcohol and Drug Abuse and Mental Illness: 1985* (Rockville, Md.: Alcohol, Drug Abuse and Mental Health Administration, 1990).
68. R. Fein, *Alcoholism in America: The Price We Pay* (Newport Beach, Calif.: CareInstitute, 1984); Sixth Special Report to the Congress on Alcohol and Health, 129; C. Culhane, NASADAD Study: "Treatment Works—If You Can Get It," *U.S. Journal of Drug and Alcohol Dependence* 14 (May 1990): 1.
69. Zook and Moore.
70. C. J. Zook, S. F. Savickis, and F. D. Moore, "Repeated Hospitalization for the Same Disease: A Multiplier of National Health Costs," *Milbank Memorial Fund Quarterly: Health and Society* 58, no. 3 (1980).
71. *Sixth Special Report to the U.S. Congress on Alcohol and Health*, 124; T. F. Kirn, "Advances in Understanding of Alcoholism Initiate Evolution in Treatment Programs," *Journal of the American Medical Association* 256 (1986): 1405, 1411.
72. D. J. Anderson, *Perspectives on Treatment: The Minnesota Experience* (Center City, Minn.: Hazelden Educational Materials, 1981), 39.
73. N. G. Hoffman and P. A. Harrison, *The Chemical Abuse/Addiction Treatment Outcome Registry (CATOR): Findings Two Years After Treatment* (1986 report); *Adolescent Residential Treatment Intake and Follow up* (St. Paul: Ramsey Clinic, Dept. of Psychiatry, 1987); J. Spicer, *Treatment Evaluation and Research* (Center City, Minn.: Hazelden Educational Materials, 1990).
74. M. A. Schuckit, "Alcoholic Hallucinosis and Paranoia," *Advances in Alcoholism* 1, Raleigh Hills Foundation (August 1980).
75. *Al-Anon Faces Alcoholism*; M. Beattie, *Codependent No More* (Center City: Hazelden Educational Materials, 1988); see *The Self-Help Sourcebook* (3d ed.) for national listings of various caregivers' self-help groups.
76. D. Callahan, "Vital Distinctions, Mortal Questions," *Commonweal* (15 July 1988): 397–404; L. Bickman and P. R. Dokecki, "Public and Private Responsibility for Mental Health Services," *American Psychologist* 44 (August 1989); 1133–37; A. Strauss and J. M. Corbin, *Shaping a New Health Care System: The Explosion of Chronic Illness as a Catalyst for Change* (San Francisco: Jossey-Bass, 1988); J. Brody, "Most Challenging Aspect of Fighting Cancer is Often Success," *Star Tribune*, 28 July 1991: 4E.
77. Callahan, 398.
78. *The Surgeon General's Workshop on Self-Help and Public Health*, 42; *The Impact of Life Threatening Conditions: Self-Help Groups and Health Care Providers in Partnership* (symposium), abstracts prepared by Minnie Bridges, AMA, Chicago, 1989.
79. H. Nouwen, *Out of Solitude* (Fides Press, 1975).

80. M. Mayeroff, *On Caring* (New York: Harper & Row, 1971).

About the Author

Damian McElrath, Ph.D., served in a variety of positions at Hazelden from 1978 until his retirement in 1995, most notably as executive vice president of Recovery Services. McElrath came to Hazelden after twenty years of teaching, counseling, and administrative work; he was president of St. Bonaventure University from 1972 to 1976. He is well known for his lectures on addiction, spirituality and the Twelve Steps and has lectured at the Rutgers Summer School of Alcohol Studies and its European branch from 1981 to 1998. He has published numerous scholarly books and articles on historical and theological topics and is the author of the Hazelden books *Hazelden: A Spiritual Odyssey* (1987), *Dan Anderson: A Biography* (1999), and *Patrick Butler: A Biography* (1999).

Hazelden Information and Educational Services, is a division of the Hazelden Foundation, a not-for-profit organization. Since 1949, Hazelden has been a leader in promoting the dignity and treatment of people afflicted with the disease of chemical dependency.

The mission of the foundation is to improve the quality of life for individuals, families, and communities by providing a national continuum of information, education, and recovery services that are widely accessible; to advance the field through research and training; and to improve our quality and effectiveness through continuous improvement and innovation.

Stemming from that, the mission of this division is to provide quality information and support to people wherever they may be in their personal journey—from education and early intervention, through treatment and recovery, to personal and spiritual growth.

Although our treatment programs do not necessarily use everything Hazelden publishes, our bibliotherapeutic materials support our mission and the Twelve Step philosophy upon which it is based. We encourage your comments and feedback.

The headquarters of the Hazelden Foundation are in Center City, Minnesota. Additional treatment facilities are located in Chicago, Illinois; New York, New York; Plymouth, Minnesota; St. Paul, Minnesota; and West Palm Beach, Florida. At these sites, we provide a continuum of care for men and women of all ages. Our Plymouth facility is designed specifically for youth and families.

For more information on Hazelden, please call **1-800-257-7800**. Or you may access our World Wide Web site on the Internet at **www.hazelden.org**.